MATH FOR SMARTY PANTS

Marilyn Burns
illustrated by Martha Weston

Little, Brown and Company
Boston   Toronto   London

To find the year this book was
written, just add any row, column, or
diagonal in the square below, or the four
corners plus the middle number.

390	403	386	394	408
396	405	392	400	388
402	385	398	407	389
409	391	399	387	395
384	397	406	393	401

This Brown Paper School book was edited and
prepared for publication at the Yolla Bolly Press,
Covelo, California, during the spring of 1981. The series
is under the supervision of James and Carolyn Robertson.
Editorial and production staff: Dan Hibshman, Barbara
Youngblood, Diana Fairbanks, and Joyca Cunnan.

Library of Congress Cataloging in Publication Data

Burns, Marilyn.
  Math for smarty pants.

(A Brown paper school book)
Summary: Text, illustrations, and suggested
activities offer a common-sense approach to
mathematic fundamentals for those who are slightly
terrified of numbers.
  1. Mathematics—1961- —Juvenile
literature. [1. Mathematics] I. Weston, Martha,
ill. II. Title.
QA40.5.B88   513   81-19314
ISBN 0-316-11738-2   AACR2
ISBN 0-316-11739-0 (pbk.)

Published simultaneously in Canada
by Little, Brown & Company (Canada) Limited.
Printed in the United States of America.

HC: 10 9 8 7 6 5 4 3
PB: 10 9 8 7

This book is dedicated
to anyone who likes the idea—
even a little bit.

What's in this book?

GETTING STARTED

What does it mean to be a mathematical smarty pants? It sounds like it means being smart in math. And it does. But that only helps if you understand what it really means to be smart in math. And that's not so simple to explain because being smart in math can mean several things, and different things.

Here's an example. There are some kids who are whizzes at dealing with numbers. They do arithmetic fast, really fast. Ask them which is a better buy, two for a nickel or three for a dime, and they've figured it out in a jiffy. (Do you know?) And not only do they know for sure whether ½ or ⅓ is larger, they can tell you fractions that fit in between those two, lots of them. (Can you?) They never seem to forget where the decimal point goes in a problem, or how many times a number goes into another. Are these kids smart in math? In a way, yes. Being smart with numbers is one way to be smart in math. But it's not the only way.

Then there are the kids who are great with shapes, who can "see" things easily in their heads. When a certain kind of problem comes along, it's just their cup of tea. For example, they can tell if a particular shape, such as this one,

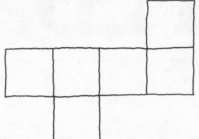

will fold up into a cube, without having to cut it out and test it. (Will it?) There may not even be numbers in the kinds of problems these kids are good at and like to do, but with anything geometric, it's a cinch. Are these kids smart in math? Yes, they're smart, in a different way than the number whizzes are.

Some kids are good at strategy games and puzzles that don't have much to do with either arithmetic or shapes, but have more to do with thinking logically to figure things out. Give them puzzles, and they're the first to find a solution. Play a game of giant tic-tac-toe with them, one with a board like this one,

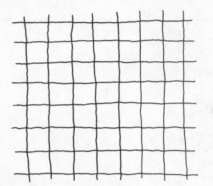

where you need four in a row to win, and they are tough to beat. Really tough.

For some kids, being fast in math is important. They like to get the right answers, in a hurry, and then get on to the next problem. Not so for others. Other kids tend to work a long time on problems, never seeming to be in a rush, and often are just as interested in seeing if there are other solutions to the same problem. Neither one of these kids is necessarily more of a mathematical smarty pants than the other.

Are You a Math Smarty Pants?

You may be wondering if you qualify as a mathematical smarty pants. You're not alone. Lots of kids wonder about that. What's important for you to realize is that mathematical smarty pants come in many types. The truth is this: You're not born being a math smarty pants—it is something you learn. The real trick to being a math smarty pants is believing that math makes sense, or *can* make sense if you put your mind to it. If you believe that, or are willing to believe it, even just a little bit, then this book can help. Believing takes practice, and the best kind of practice is math practice. There's plenty of that in this book. You can be a mathematical smarty pants if you really want to. It's up to you.

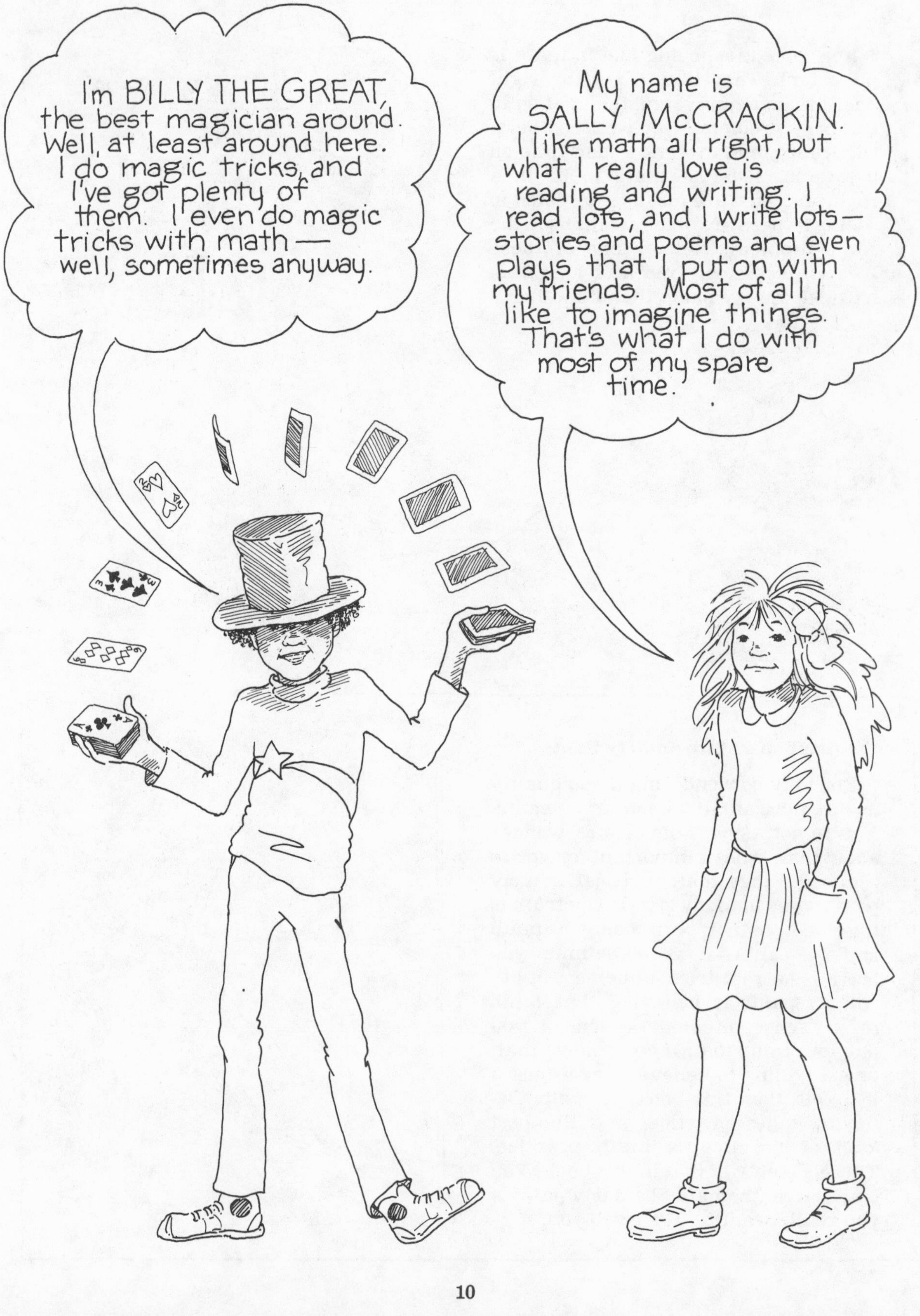
I'm BILLY THE GREAT, the best magician around. Well, at least around here. I do magic tricks, and I've got plenty of them. I even do magic tricks with math— well, sometimes anyway.
My name is SALLY McCRACKIN. I like math all right, but what I really love is reading and writing. I read lots, and I write lots— stories and poems and even plays that I put on with my friends. Most of all I like to imagine things. That's what I do with most of my spare time.

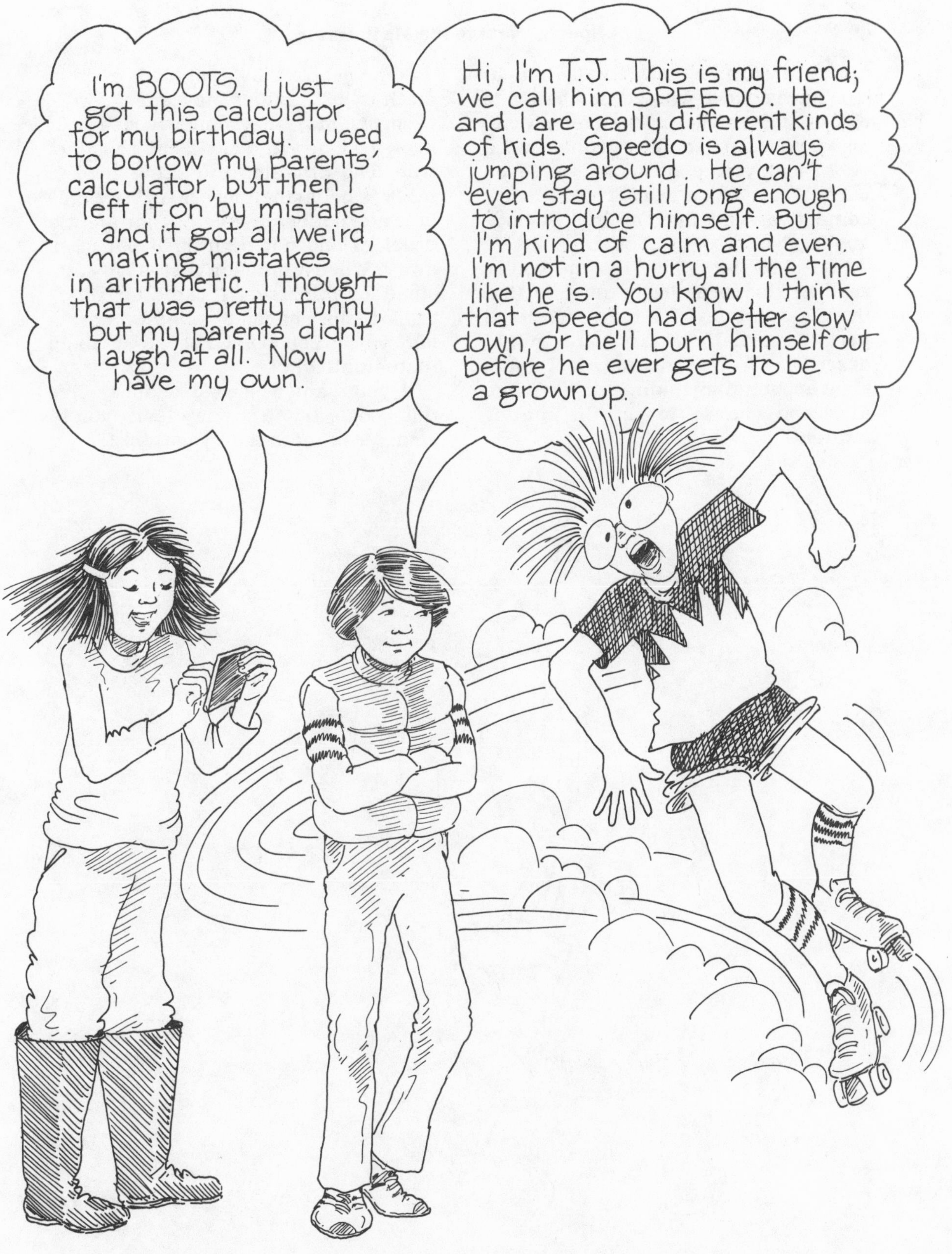
I'm BOOTS. I just got this calculator for my birthday. I used to borrow my parents' calculator, but then I left it on by mistake and it got all weird, making mistakes in arithmetic. I thought that was pretty funny, but my parents didn't laugh at all. Now I have my own.
Hi, I'm T.J. This is my friend; we call him SPEEDO. He and I are really different kinds of kids. Speedo is always jumping around. He can't even stay still long enough to introduce himself. But I'm kind of calm and even. I'm not in a hurry all the time like he is. You know, I think that Speedo had better slow down, or he'll burn himself out before he ever gets to be a grownup.

A Special Note to the Math Hater

Maybe you hate math. Really hate it. You have no idea whether it's better to buy two for a nickel or three for a dime, or whether any shape will fold into a cube, and you're not sure you even care. What you're wondering is: How come I've read this far in this book anyway?

Consider this: The reason you're reading this book right now is that there's a part of you, a mere fractional part (as a math smarty pants might describe it), that doesn't feel quite right about hating math. And you'd like a second chance to set the matter straight.

Some people think that being good in math is just getting the right answers to problems; they think you either know how or you don't. That's just not true. The first step in getting good in math is believing there is a difference between not being able to figure out a problem and not figuring it out right away. When a problem seems hard, instead of thinking "I can't do this," think "I just haven't solved this problem yet." You don't need to rush in mathematics!

If you want a second chance, give this book a try. You may learn you're smarter in math than you think!

PART 1
Arithmetic with a Twist

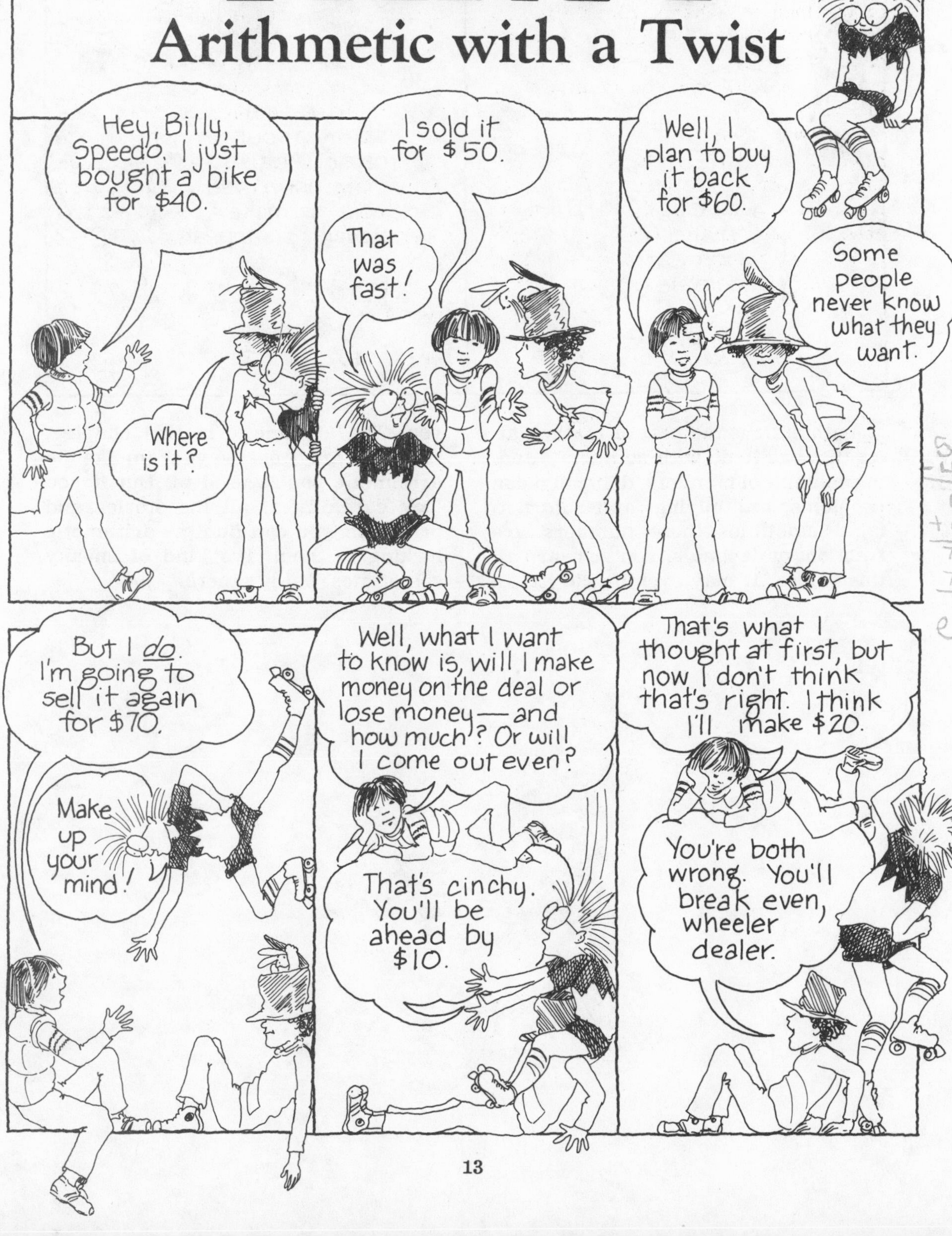

Hey, Billy, Speedo. I just bought a bike for $40.
Where is it?
I sold it for $50.
That was fast!
Well, I plan to buy it back for $60.
Some people never know what they want.
But I do. I'm going to sell it again for $70.
Make up your mind!
Well, what I want to know is, will I make money on the deal or lose money—and how much? Or will I come out even?
That's cinchy. You'll be ahead by $10.
That's what I thought at first, but now I don't think that's right. I think I'll make $20.
You're both wrong. You'll break even, wheeler dealer.

Arithmetic is the part of mathematics that has to do with numbers—adding columns of numbers, doing division problems, multiplying, and subtracting. Sometimes those numbers are fractions or decimals. You've heard all this before. It may even be old hat to you. The arithmetic in this chapter, however, may not always seem like the arithmetic you're used to. But if you look carefully at all the stories and problems, you can find the arithmetic lurking in them. It's kind of sneaky sometimes, but it's there.

The $1 Word Search

"Excellent" is a $1 word, mathematically speaking. So is "discipline," which is what you'll need to find more of these wonders. To find them give each letter a cent value: a = 1 cent, b = 2 cents, c = 3 cents, and so on up to z = 26 cents. Then add the value of each letter in a word. Check for yourself to see that "excellent" and "discipline" really are $1 words. Now it's up to you. How about your first name? Is it worth $1? ("Suzanne" and "Kristin" are. So are "Henrietta" and "Christian.")

To help in your search for more of these valuable words, here are some hints. There is a Halloween word that is worth $1. (Nope, it's not "Halloween"; that's worth only 95 cents.) There's a Thanksgiving $1 word, as well as one astrological sign and one U.S. coin. There are at least two U.S. cities—one is in Wisconsin, and the other is in both Oregon and Maine.

There's a beverage that is illegal for kids to drink that's worth $1, though it sometimes costs more than that to buy it in restaurants and bars. There are several animals at the zoo that are $1 words, and one underwater creature. There's a number less than 100 that's worth $1, as well as something you wear to keep your hands warm in the winter.

At this time more than 200 $1 words have been discovered by addition-loving kids from all over the United States. How about having a $1 word contest at your next party? And if you read carefully through this book, you'll find $1 sentences stuck in from time to time—sentences in which every word is worth $1.00!

Here's a paradox!* *Gold* is worth only 38¢, but *silver* is 75¢!

How much is *Weldon the Magic Bunny* worth?

A *dollar* is worth only 62¢.

My Uncle 'Roy says it isn't even worth that much.

Plenty, Buster.

* What's a paradox? See page 81.

★ $1 SENTENCE ★

Filtering upsets smokers.

15

Mathematical Stunt Flying

Mathematicians have their own version of stunt flying. (Wouldn't you know it!) They use numbers instead of airplanes. They get their thrills from numerical loopings and from discovering patterns while they're doing their tricks. One person's pattern is another's loop-the-loop.

Looping — 4-2-1-4-2-1-4-2-1-4.

NUMBER 1. Start with any number you like and follow these rules. If the number you start with is even, divide it in half. If it's odd, multiply it by 3, then add 1. Whatever answer you get, apply one of these rules to it again. And do that over and over again—that's the looping part.

Here's a sample. Start with 10. It's even, so take half. That gives you 5. That's odd, so multiply it by 3 and add 1: $(5 \times 3) + 1 = 16$. Back to even, so take half and get 8. Half again gives you 4. Half again gets you to 2, and half again gives you 1. Since 1 is odd, multiply by 3 and add 1 to get 4. Half of 4 gives you 2, and half of that gets you back to 1. You're in a loop now and will be forever if you keep at it.

Try the same procedure with 30 and see if what you get matches this: 30, 15, 46, 23, 70, 35, 106, 53, 160, 80, 40, 20, 10, 5, 16, 8, 4, 2, 1, 4, 2, 1.

Try a few more. If you start with 88, you'll have 17 steps to go before you hit 1. If you start with 27, it takes 109

steps! With a calculator, you should be able to poke right along; without one, you'll still get there—it will just take a while longer.

Here goes **3**. It's **odd**, so I'll multiply it by 3, which makes 9. Add 1, that gives me **10**. That's even, so I

divide it in half and get **5**. That's **odd**, so I multiply it by 3, which

makes 15, plus 1 is **16**. Back to even, so half of

Hmm.... Looks familiar already.

This system for looping interests mathematicians. In fact, it has interested some mathematicians so much that they've tried starting with every number from 1 to 1,000. Every one loops into that 4—2—1 pattern at the end.

Mathematicians are never satisfied, and the question they have is this: Will every number loop into that pattern? Well, there's no telling. It's not possible to figure out a proof. A proof is an explanation that convinces everyone that something is true without their having to try it over and over again. As clever as mathematicians are, not one of them has come up with a proof that looping back to 4—2—1 will always happen. No one has found a number that doesn't work, but no one has been able to prove that *any* number will work. It just goes to show that mathematicians don't know everything.

Looping 8—9—7—6—3—9—2—1—3—4—7

NUMBER 2.
For this numerical stunt, you start with any two numbers from 0 to 9 and follow this rule: Add the two numbers and write down just the digit that is in the ones place. Here's an example: Suppose you start with 8 and 9. Adding them gives you 17. Keep just the 7, which is in the ones place. So now you have 8—9—7. Add the last two numbers, the 9 and the 7. That gives 16; keep just the 6, then you have 8—9—7—6. Keep going, adding the last two numbers in the series each time, keeping only the digit in the ones place. Do this until you get 8 and 9 again. Then the loop starts all over. The 8—9 pattern has twelve numbers in the loop before it repeats.

If going around in a numerical circle appeals to you, you may have the makings of a terrific mathematician. Hang in there. But beware. If you start with the same two numbers, but in the opposite order, and follow the same rule: 9—8—7—5, and so on, it will take 60 numbers before it starts to repeat! Don't tackle that one unless you're sure you have the time. For a quickie, start with 2 and 6.

Here are the kinds of questions mathematicians ask about an exploration such as this one: How many different possible pairs of numbers are there to start with? (It's okay to start with two numbers that are the same.) What's the shortest loop you can find? What's the longest loop? Is there a pattern of odds and evens in the loop?

Looping 4-four-4-four-4-

NUMBER 3. This is a numerical looping that also uses words. You start with any number, 39, for example. Write it as a word: thirty-nine. Then continue as shown.

Start with any number	39
Write it as a word	thirty-nine
Count the letters	10
Write that as a word	ten
Count the letters	3
Write that as a word	three
Count the letters	5
Write that as a word	five
Count the letters	4
Write that as a word	four
Count the letters	4

You'll get 4 forever and ever now. As a matter of mathematical fact, you'll get to 4, no matter what number you start with originally. Try a different number and see. Convince yourself with some examples, then see if you can figure out why you'll always get to four.

Dealing in Wheeling

Have you figured out the problem T.J. presented to Billy and Speedo? If not, here's a hint. Try solving this one first; it's an identical problem: A kid bought a tape recorder for $40, then she sold it for $50; she later bought a record player for $60, then she sold it for $70.

Now you may think this isn't much of a hint. As a matter of fact, you may think the two problems are not identical at all. Well, they are. Don't let the bicycle part in T.J.'s version throw you off the track. You have to see beyond that to get into the mathematics of this.

This problem has caused fierce arguments in Berea, Ohio, in Smithtown, New York, and in Mill Valley, California. So beware if you ask for help.

Consecutive numbers are numbers in order...

...like when I pile the cards on top of the aces in solitaire.

The Pattern of Consecutive Sums

Looking for patterns is a mathematician's idea of a swell time. It's like hunting for treasure that you know is there, if you can just unearth it. Sometimes patterns appear in the most obvious places. Even in easy addition.

Here's an addition investigation that is a problem with some interesting patterns lurking in it. This investigation has to do with writing numbers as the sum of consecutive numbers. Consecutive numbers are numbers that go in order—like 1, 2, 3 or 29, 30, 31, 32 or 745, 746—and don't skip to get from one to the next. So 6, 8, 9 aren't consecutive because the 7 was skipped. And 1, 3, 5, 7 aren't because with them you need to add two to get from one to the next.

Here's a sample of how to write a number as the sum of consecutives: $9 = 4 + 5$. But 9 can also be done another way: $9 = 2 + 3 + 4$.

The number 12 can only be done one way: $12 = 3 + 4 + 5$. The number 15, however, can be written as the sum of consecutive numbers in three different ways: $15 = 1 + 2 + 3 + 4 + 5$, $15 = 7 + 8$, $15 = 4 + 5 + 6$.

Your job in this investigation is to find all the possible ways to write each of the numbers from 1 to 25 as the sum of consecutives, using only whole numbers: 1, 2, 3, 4, and so on. Look for patterns. Which can be written as the sum of only two consecutives? Which can be written as the sum of three consecutive numbers? Four? More? Between 1 and 25 there are five that can't be done at all; what are they and what are their patterns? The patterns can be found everywhere, if you just know how to look.

P.S. The number 315 can be written as the sum of consecutive numbers 11 different ways; 315 is the smallest number with that characteristic.

Answer to *Dealing in Wheeling*:
It comes out $20 ahead.

Chummy Numbers

When two numbers are friends in mathematics, they are called "amicable." Take 220 and 284. There's a pair of very buddy-buddy numbers. You may be wondering why they're so friendly. (I certainly hope you're wondering. Curiosity about such matters is the first step toward becoming chummy with mathematics.)

If you add up each of those strings of numbers, you will find that the divisors of 220 add up to 284, and the divisors of 284 add up to 220. Pretty chummy, wouldn't you say? And definitely unusual.

There aren't many numbers that are such tight friends as these. Maybe that's why numbers such as these were once thought to be mystical.

Well, here's why. The numbers smaller than 220 that divide into it evenly are 1, 2, 4, 5, 10, 11, 20, 22, 44, 55, and 110. And the numbers smaller than 284 that divide into it evenly are 1, 2, 4, 71, and 142.

An Italian named Nicolo Paganini found a pair of amicable numbers when he was just 16 years old—1,184 and 1,210. Doublecheck his work. Do you agree with him? Two other pairs were found in the seventeenth century —17,296 and 18,416, and 9,363,584 and 9,437,056.

Do you have any idea how someone would set out to find a pair of amicable numbers?

The Three Little Pig Eyes

Have you heard about the three little pig eyes? These are legendary, mischievous creatures, tricksters really, who are fair in their hearts, but who spend much of their free time playing tricks on people. And they play many tricks since practically all of their time is free time. It's one of the advantages of being a legendary creature.

The magical, mischievous pig eyes are not quite as well known as some other fabled creatures. Or maybe they are just not as popular. Perhaps it's because they have hideous, annoying laughs. They're either laughing at their own jokes, jokes that no one else would think are at all funny, or they're laughing at other people, who weren't even making jokes.

Here's an example of the kind of trick they play, one that they thought was really funny. They played this trick on Sally McCrackin, who didn't think it was funny at all. That's usually the way with their tricks.

Sally McCrackin was walking home from school one day. She had just said goodby to her best friend, Lisa, and was walking the last stretch alone, reaching into her school bag for the sack of peanuts she was saving for this part of the walk. (Sally loves peanuts.) She had the sack in her hand and was about to reach in for her first peanut. Suddenly, from the side of the road, out jumped one of the tricksters with little pig eyes.

"Peanuts, huh!" the trickster cried. "Oh, how I love peanuts," and it grabbed Sally's sack right out of her hand.

"Give me that!" Sally shouted. "You have no business grabbing a kid's sack of peanuts. They're mine, and you'd better give them back to me."

The trickster laughed one of those hideous laughs, and that's when Sally got a little scared.

"You can have a few if you like," she said a little nervously.

"I can have as many as I like," replied the trickster, "but I feel pretty generous today. I'll just take half of them." And it dumped out the peanuts, dividing them into two equal piles. Sally watched, feeling astonished and helpless. It stuffed one pile into its pocket. Then it put the rest back into Sally's sack. "And," the beady-eyed creature said, "I think I'll take just two more from your sack." Which it did, throwing the sack back to Sally, and then disappeared behind a tree.

Sally was stunned. And wouldn't you be? She stood there for a minute, holding her sack, with the ringing of that laughter still in her head. Then she began to walk on again, a bit shaken. What else could she do?

A little farther on, when Sally was feeling a bit better and her heart wasn't pounding so hard and her breathing seemed calmer, she decided to chalk up the experience as one of life's hard knocks. She reached into the sack to cheer herself up with one of the remaining peanuts.

But even before she could eat one peanut, another of the little pig eyes jumped into her path. "Eeeaaahhh!" it screamed. The scream turned into screeching laughter when the little pig eyes grabbed the sack right out of Sally's hand. "I looooove peanuts."

As you might imagine, Sally was stunned. What an unlucky day this was turning out to be. But, finally, she shook herself into action and spoke with the voice she had learned to use when her dog was misbehaving. "Give me that sack of peanuts *right now,*" she said, stamping her foot.

This made the trickster laugh so hard that tears were pouring out of what seemed like the tiniest eyes Sally had ever seen. "I'll give them to you when I'm ready. Gooooood and ready. But first I'll take some for myself, if you please, or even if you don't please. I'll take half, I think." Then this little pig eyes dumped the peanuts out, dividing them into two piles, stuffing one pile into its pocket, and put the rest in Sally's sack. "And," it said, laughing so hard it had to hold its stomach, or what seemed to be its stomach, "I'll take just twooooo more and be on my way." Which it did, leaving Sally's sack on the ground, and disappeared into the field on the side of the road.

Now Sally was a very reasonable person who liked to make sense of things. But this was a tough one to figure. She didn't feel afraid exactly. She felt more startled, like she did when a mouse caught her by surprise or when a snake appeared in the road. These piggy tricksters were very unusual, bizarre even, but they didn't seem dangerous. Just wait until I tell Lisa, she thought, as she picked up her sack. But would Lisa believe this? Was it really happening? Who were these creatures, with their little pig eyes and their grating laughter. They certainly are rude, she thought, whatever they are. And not knowing what else to do, Sally walked on, reaching into her sack for one of the remaining peanuts.

As you may have already guessed, Sally didn't get that peanut out of the sack. Trickster number three popped out. This one was a fast-stepping, finger-snapping weirdo who did not seem to be able to remain still for even an instant. It hopped around Sally, snapping its fingers, clapping its hands, talking as fast as it moved. "Peanuts, peanuts, I love peanuts. And most of all, I love your peanuts. Do not dawdle, my little sweet. Hand over the sack, the entire treat."

This time Sally got mad, really mad. "Don't call me your little sweet. I'm not your little anything, and I know what you want. You want half my peanuts, then two more, and I think that's mean. And I think you're weird and ridiculous looking, and you probably have a hideous laugh."

That seemed to be the funniest thing the trickster had ever heard, judging from the way it fell to the ground laughing and shrieking, grabbing the sack at the same time. "You're right, my clever peanut lover," it said, turning somersaults. "Half plus two more, that's for me; a more cooperative Sally there will never be. A pile for me, a pile for you, then I'll reach in your sack and also take two." Off it ran, running with a strange gait, clicking its heels, swinging its arms over its head.

All this was too much for Sally. She had been brave up to this point, but now she'd had too much. She sat down at the side of the road, clutching her sack. She opened it up and looked inside. There were only two peanuts left. Only two peanuts. A little while ago her sack had been full. Sally put her face in her hands and started to cry, loud, jerking, long, hard sobs. Finally she stopped crying, gasping for breath, and reached in her pocket for a handkerchief to dry her eyes. She looked up, and there in front of her were the three creatures, not laughing at all now, but lined up staring at her.

Sally tried staring back at them but could feel herself beginning to cry again. She tried to control herself; she hated having them see how upset they made her. "You're mean!" she said to them, raising her chin a little.

"We're just tricksters," the first one answered.

"Hrrummff," Sally said, still sniffling.

"It was just a trick we played. That's what we do; we play tricks on people," the second one said.

"You took my peanuts, that's what you did," Sally accused.

"We'll give them back to you if that will make you feel better," the third one said.

Sally looked at them suspiciously. "Prove it," she said.

The three huddled together in a group, whispering to each other. Sally sat there, unable to hear what they were saying and very tired of the entire situation. She wanted to get her peanuts back and to go home and forget the whole thing.

The three came out of their huddle.

"We've agreed to return all your peanuts to you," the first one said.

"But we have decided that we'll do this only if you can figure out a problem," said the second one.

"Oh, no," Sally said, rolling her eyes. "Now what do you want?"

"Well," the fast-talking third creature said, "playing tricks is our favorite thing to do, and we're good at it."

"So I've noticed," Sally commented.

"But," it went on, ignoring her, "sometimes playing tricks isn't very nice, and we know that, so we substitute being tricky for playing a trick. We've got a tricky problem for you, and if you can solve it, you'll get every peanut back. Honest."

"Why not just give me the peanuts?" Sally asked. "They are mine, you know."

"We can't do that," the second trickster explained. "Since we're tricksters, we have to have some fun. Being tricky is allllllmost as much fun as playing tricks."

"Would you like to hear the problem?" the first little pig eyes asked.

"Oh, all right," Sally replied. "What is your tricky problem?"

They answered in unison. "How many peanuts were in your sack when it was full?"

"I don't know," Sally said.

"That's the problem," the first one said, giggling a little.

"You can figure it out. You know we each took half plus two more," the second one said, starting to giggle also.

"And you have two left in the sack," the third one said. And the three of them began rolling on the ground, laughing and laughing.

Sally ignored their laughing and began to think. After a while she got out some paper and a pencil and wrote some figures. Then she collected some pebbles to use as the peanuts. She actually got interested in the problem. And, sure enough, she solved it.

As soon as Sally announced her answer to the three little pig eyes, they emptied their pockets and counted up to see if she was right. She was, and they put all the peanuts back into her sack, gave it to her, and scampered away, laughing as if this were the funniest thing they had ever done.

What answer did Sally come up with?

Like many math problems, this one can be solved in several different ways. It is a tricky problem since it seems as if it has to do with arithmetic, but not the usual arithmetic. It's not a "trick" problem, like the "What's Odd About This?" problem on page 86. Tricky problems are fair and square, but trick problems have a sneaky twist that can stump even the best mathematical thinkers. Discuss this problem with someone else to see if you can find different ways to solve it.

On Which Day of the Week Were You Born?

Even though you were there at the time, you may not know on which day of the week you were born. Your parents may remember; then again they may not. (You never can be sure what grownups will remember.) With some careful mathematics, however, it's possible to figure out on which day you were born. Just follow these directions.

When were these pig eyes you met born?

I don't think they *have* birthdays!

1. Write the last two digits of the year you were born. Call this number A.

2. Divide that number (A) by 4 and drop the remainder if there is one. This answer, without the remainder, is B.

3. Find the number for the month in which you were born in the Table of Months below. Call this number C.

4. On which date of the month were you born? Call this number D.

5. Add the numbers from each of the first four steps: A + B + C + D.

6. Divide the sum you got in step 5 by the number 7. What is the remainder from that division? (It should be a number from 0 to 6.) Find this remainder in the Table of Days. That table tells you on which day of the week you were born.

This method works for any date, as long as it's in the twentieth century. You can't use it to find out days before 1900. It *will* help you find out on which day of the week Halloween or your next birthday will land. In the back of some telephone books there is a perpetual calendar. That calendar will help you check to see if you did your mathematics correctly.

TABLE OF MONTHS	
JANUARY	1 (0 in a leap year)
FEBRUARY	4 (3 in a leap year)
MARCH	4
APRIL	0
MAY	2
JUNE	5
JULY	0
AUGUST	3
SEPTEMBER	6
OCTOBER	1
NOVEMBER	4
DECEMBER	6

TABLE OF DAYS	
SUNDAY	1
MONDAY	2
TUESDAY	3
WEDNESDAY	4
THURSDAY	5
FRIDAY	6
SATURDAY	0

Have you ever heard the Mother Goose rhyme, "Solomon Grundy"? Here's one version of it:

> Solomon Grundy
> Born on Monday
> Christened on Tuesday
> Married on Wednesday
> Took ill on Thursday
> Worse on Friday
> Died on Saturday
> Buried on Sunday
> This is the end
> Of Solomon Grundy.

How is that possible? With a bit of logical thinking, it's possible to explain how the life of Solomon Grundy really could have happened as the rhyme says it did. It's surprising how often mathematical thinking is useful.

I wonder if that rhyme has anything to do with years?

Answer to *The Three Little Pig Eyes*:
Molly started off in her sack.

★ $1 SENTENCE ★

Whenever wizards whistled, elephants spouted.

Incredible Calculators

Have you ever noticed that some people can do arithmetic faster than others can? Sometimes this is because one person has had more practice than another. But some people can do arithmetic computations so incredibly fast that practice doesn't honestly explain their abilities.

Throughout history there have been lightning-fast calculators who could do remarkable arithmetic feats in their heads. Their talents have amazed the slowpokes around them. Thomas Fuller was called the "Virginia Calculator." He was captured and brought to America from Africa as a slave in 1724, when he was only 14 years old. It wasn't until he was 70 that he became well known for his arithmetic talent. He could easily perform feats such as multiplying two nine-digit numbers in his head. Once, when his rare ability was being tested, he was asked to figure out how many seconds there were in the 70 years and 17 days he had been alive. He figured it out in a minute and a half—in his head. The examiners who were testing him figured the answer also—on paper, of course. They got a different answer. But Thomas Fuller was able to show them that they had forgotten about leap years! Thomas Fuller died in 1790 at the age of 80, never having had any formal schooling and without even learning to read or write.

••-→-←-••

Zerah Colburn was the son of a farmer. He was born in Vermont in 1804. His parents never thought he was very bright, but after he had been in school for only a month and a half, they heard him reciting parts of the multiplication tables. His father, curious about his son's interest in multiplication, asked Zerah, "How much is 13 x 97?" "1,261," Zerah answered, as quickly as *you* might give the answer to 3 x 5. Zerah was only six years old at the time. Zerah's father immediately took Zerah out of school and on an exhibition tour with high hopes of earning lots of money by showing off his son's remarkable talent.

"flew around the room like a top, pulling his pantaloons over the tops of his boots, biting his hands, rolling his eyes in their sockets, sometimes smiling and talking, and then seeming to be in agony." In less than one minute, he had come up with the correct answer: 133,491,850,208,566,925,016,658,299,941,583,225! Truman admitted that he was tired after doing this calculation. Truman never did public exhibitions. He eventually went to college and studied astronomy; but as he got older, he lost some of the amazing abilities he had had when he was young. He died in 1901.

At the age of eight, when Zerah was giving a demonstration of his powers in England, he was asked to compute 8 to the 16th power. That means 8 x 8 x 8 x 8 and so on, multiplying 8 by itself 16 times. He gave the answer, which is 281,474,976,710,656, quickly and easily and brought the astounded audience to tears.

Zerah received his formal education in England. With education, strangely, his calculating abilities decreased. Eventually he returned to the United States, where he tried acting and schoolmastering, becoming a preacher and later a teacher of Greek, Latin, French, Spanish, and English. He wrote his autobiography, explaining some of his calculating methods. Zerah Colburn died in 1840.

·-·-⋝·⋜-·-·

Another calculating prodigy, Truman Henry Safford, was born in 1836, also in Vermont. When he was ten years old, the Reverend H. W. Adam gave him this problem: Multiply in your head 365,365,365,365,365,365 x 365,365,365,365,365. According to Reverend Adam's description, Truman

There have been others with these incredible calculating abilities. If these stories were interesting to you, you may want to find out about other arithmetic prodigies. Ask a librarian for help in finding information about John Wallis; Johann Carl Friedrich Gauss; Andre Marie Ampere; George Parker Bidder, Sr.; George Parker Bidder, Jr.; Johann Martin; Zacharias Dase; Jacques Inaudi; and Shakuntale Devi.

Speedo Multiplication

Some of the people who have been famous calculating whizzes have been able to explain some shortcuts. It's unlikely that you'll be able to match their extraordinary feats, but you can learn some calculating tricks and dazzle your friends and family. You may even dazzle yourself.

Most calculating shortcuts require that you do some mental arithmetic, and often keep some figures in your memory. Here's a speedo way to multiply any number by 11. Try this method to see if you can get good at it and if you like this sort of thing. It may seem complicated to learn, but once you do, it's really fast.

When you multiply a number by 11, using this method, you get your answer one digit at a time, starting in the ones place and moving to the left. Here's an example: 523 x 11.

1. The ones digit of the answer is the same as the ones digit of the number you're multiplying by 11: 3.

2. To get the tens digit of the answer, look at the tens digit in the number: 2. Add that to its right-hand neighbor (the 3 in the ones place): 2 + 3 = 5. That's the tens digit in the answer. Now you have 53.

3. Continue the same way. To find the next digit of the answer, find the digit in the same place in the number and add it to its right-hand neighbor. The answer so far: 753.

4. The farthest left-hand digit in the answer is the left-hand digit in the number. The final answer using this method is 5,753. Do you agree?

33

Write down a few more "times 11" problems, and you'll start to see why this shortcut works.

Sometimes when you add a number to its right-hand neighbor, that sum is more than 9, so you have to carry 1, just like in regular addition. For example, if you use this method to calculate 892 x 11, you'll have to carry 1's.

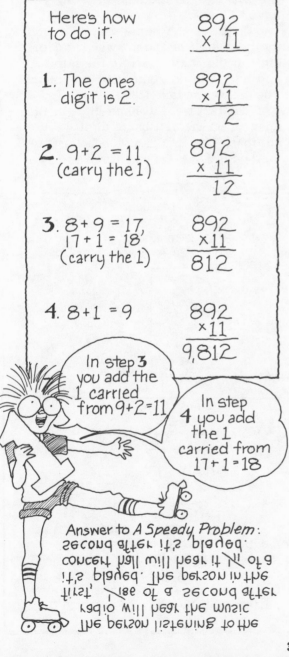

Here's how to do it.

$$892 \times 11$$

1. The ones digit is 2.

$$892 \times 11 \over 2$$

2. 9 + 2 = 11 (carry the 1)

$$892 \times 11 \over 12$$

3. 8 + 9 = 17, 17 + 1 = 18, (carry the 1)

$$892 \times 11 \over 812$$

4. 8 + 1 = 9

$$892 \times 11 \over 9,812$$

In step 3 you add the 1 carried from 9 + 2 = 11

In step 4 you add the 1 carried from 17 + 1 = 18

To multiply by 12, the method is almost the same as for multiplying by 11. The difference is that you double the digit before adding its right-hand neighbor to it (except for the final digit). So to multiply 564 x 12, follow these steps:

1. To get the ones digit, double the ones digit in the number you're multiplying by 12: 8.

2. For the next digit in the answer, take the 6 and double it, then add it to its right-hand neighbor: 12 + 4 = 16. Write the 6 and carry the 1; now you have 68.

3. For the next digit, take the 5 in the number, double it, then add it to its right-hand neighbor, which is 6: 10 + 6 = 16. Then add the 1 you carried from the previous addition to get 17. Write the 7 and carry the 1. This gives you 768.

4. The left-hand digit of the answer is the same as the left-hand digit in the problem, but you have to add the 1 you've carried, so it's 6. The final answer is 6,768. Check it.

There are tricks for doing other calculations as well. If you are interested, check in the library for books about arithmetic shortcuts.

Answer to *A Speedy Problem*:
The person listening to the music will hear the music first. It's played a second after it is played. The person in the concert hall will hear it 1/5 of a second after it's played.

Upside-Down Riddles

You might think that your calculator can only communicate with numbers. But you can get it to flash words too. Punch in numbers, then turn your calculator upside down to see if you made a word. To get the idea, punch in 3045, turn your calculator upside down, and read SHOE. Try 35009818 and read BIG GOOSE.

Now you add the riddle part. You get a riddle and a clue. Riddle: What do you do in rain puddles? Clue: 15025 x 3. Try it to see if you get the answer SLOSH.

Here are some more. What sound does a turkey make? (18403 x 2 + 3). What surrounds a baby chick before it hatches? (1546686 x 5 + 12563). What kind of pop is good to lick? (53121 ÷ 3).

Answer to *The Million-Dollar Giveaway*:
It would take 20,000 hours
Big news every million dollars to
step out that's over two years.

The Eights Have It

$$9 \times 9 + 7 = 88$$
$$9 \times 98 + 6 = 888$$
$$9 \times 987 + 5 = 8{,}888$$
$$? = ?$$

Can you continue the pattern?

What Comes Next?

Figure out what's happening here, then see if the pattern continues.

$$1 \times 8 + 1 = 9$$
$$12 \times 8 + 2 = 98$$
$$123 \times 8 + 3 = 987$$
$$1{,}234 \times 8 + 4 = 9{,}876$$

These patterns really begin in the good, old multiplication tables. Write down the 8's and the 9's in vertical columns, and you'll see where the fancy patterns get their start.

Divisibility

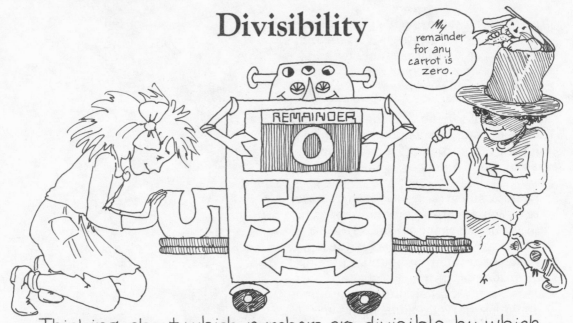

My remainder for any carrot is zero.

Thinking about which numbers are divisible by which others is a topic that interests mathematicians. For one number to be divisible by another means that it can be divided by it with no leftovers; the remainder is zero.

2

For a number to be divisible by 2, for example, it has to be even. Numbers such as 8, 10, 64, and 2,368 are divisible by 2; 5, 67, and 103 aren't. So you can tell whether a number is divisible by 2 just by looking to see if it's even. You don't actually have to do the division.

3

Deciding if a number is divisible by 3, however, isn't so obvious. Take 144, for example. You can't tell just by looking whether 3 will go into 144 with no remainder or not. You could find out by dividing, but there's another way. To test if a number is divisible by 3, add up the digits in the number you're testing. Is that sum divisible by 3? Take 144, for

example: If you add 1 + 4 + 4, you get 9. Since 9 is divisible by 3, so is 144. Not so with 145. If you add 1 + 4 + 5, you get 10, which isn't divisible by 3, so neither is 145. You can check these on your calculator. This test is useful for large numbers such as 273,645. Add the digits: 2 + 7 + 3 + 6 + 4 + 5. The sum is 27. Still not sure? Then add the 2 and the 7. That should convince you.

4

For divisibility by 4, you can test by looking at the last two digits of the number you're testing. If that number is divisible by 4, so is the entire number. This works well for large numbers such as 2,365,716. The last two digits are 16, which is divisible by 4. Check with your calculator to see if the larger number is also.

5

You can go back to the "look" method to test for divisibility by 5. Any number that ends in 0 or 5 is divisible by 5. That's easy.

6

See if you can figure a divisibility test for dividing by 6. Hint: You have to combine two of the tests given so far.

7

A really tricky situation is the test for divisibility by 7. A weird 3—2—1 pattern helps here. For example, to test an enormous number, such as 6,124,314, you have to figure like this: 3 x the ones digit + (2 x the tens digit) - (1 x the hundreds digit) - (3 x the thousands digit) - (2 x the ten thousands digit) + (1 x the hundred thousands digit) + (3 x the millions digit). Try the test on 6,124,314, then check your test by actually dividing it out—with a calculator if you'd like. Then use part of the test to show that 18,102 is divisible by 7. (Watch the + and - signs.)

Okay, divide me up!

You might be thinking that it's easier just to divide, rather than go through such a complicated test. Maybe so. But for some people, thinking about the tests is lots more fun than doing the division, with or without a calculator. Some people will spend a long time— once—looking for a shortcut they can use forever.

Try this **Fraction Fooler**, little Demi What's one-half of one-half divided by one-half?

Is anything left??

Answer to Ice Cream and the Three Little Pig Eyes:

—billy g ate 6 #5 ate a cone, netsa-chocolate billy cone, netsa-chocolate cone, chocolate cone

The Calculator Argument

Once upon a time two mathematicians were having a discussion. An argument, really. "Calculators are terrific arithmetic tools," said one of the mathematicians.

"I agree," said the other. (That wasn't what the argument was about.)

The first mathematician went on. "I wonder why they even bother to make kids learn how to do arithmetic with paper and pencil. Why don't all kids just get a calculator along with all their other school supplies?"

"*What?*" said the second mathematician. That's when the argument started. "That's crazy. Having a calculator to use is a convenience, I agree, but it doesn't replace knowing how to do something on your own."

"Why should kids have to learn how to do something that they never have to do, something that a calculator can always be used for?" the first mathematician answered.

"Why should kids not have the advantage of knowing how to do arithmetic? It would be like having to carry an extra brain around in their pockets. What if they had to do some figuring and didn't have their calculators with them? Or what if the batteries were dead? What about that?" The argument was getting serious.

"No one is ever in that much of a rush. Doing arithmetic is never an emergency situation. Having to wait to get a new battery would seem to take less time than all the time it would take to learn and practice how to do arithmetic. That takes years to do, years that kids could spend doing much more interesting things in math."

"Look," the second mathematician went on, exasperated, "kids need to learn to be self-sufficient, to be able to depend on themselves to do jobs. Using a calculator isn't bad; it just shouldn't be the only way kids can do arithmetic. It just doesn't make sense."

The first mathematician wouldn't budge in the argument. "The calculator is a tool. When you do a job, it makes sense to use the best tool there is to do that job. If you have a pencil sharpener, you don't use a knife to sharpen a pencil. If you're in a hurry, you don't walk; you go by car. You don't walk just because it is the way you always got there, just because that was the way people used to travel."

"Aha!" answered the second mathematician. "Walking is still useful. You knew how to do that before you learned how to drive or ride a bicycle. Just because we have cars, we don't discourage kids from learning how to walk. That's a ridiculous argument."

Their argument went on and on. And on. And to this day, it hasn't been resolved. So kids still are learning how to do arithmetic. And they're also learning how to use calculators. What about you? Which mathematician do you agree with?

Let's just hope they take a break for dinner.

This argument was made up, but it's like those that many grownups are having about what to do with kids and calculators. Probably you don't have a choice; you have to learn how to do arithmetic. That's that. In the meantime, you also can learn to use your calculator. Learning to use a tool is a good idea, and there are lots of chances in this book for you to do just that. Keep an eye out for them.

PART 2
The Shapes of Math

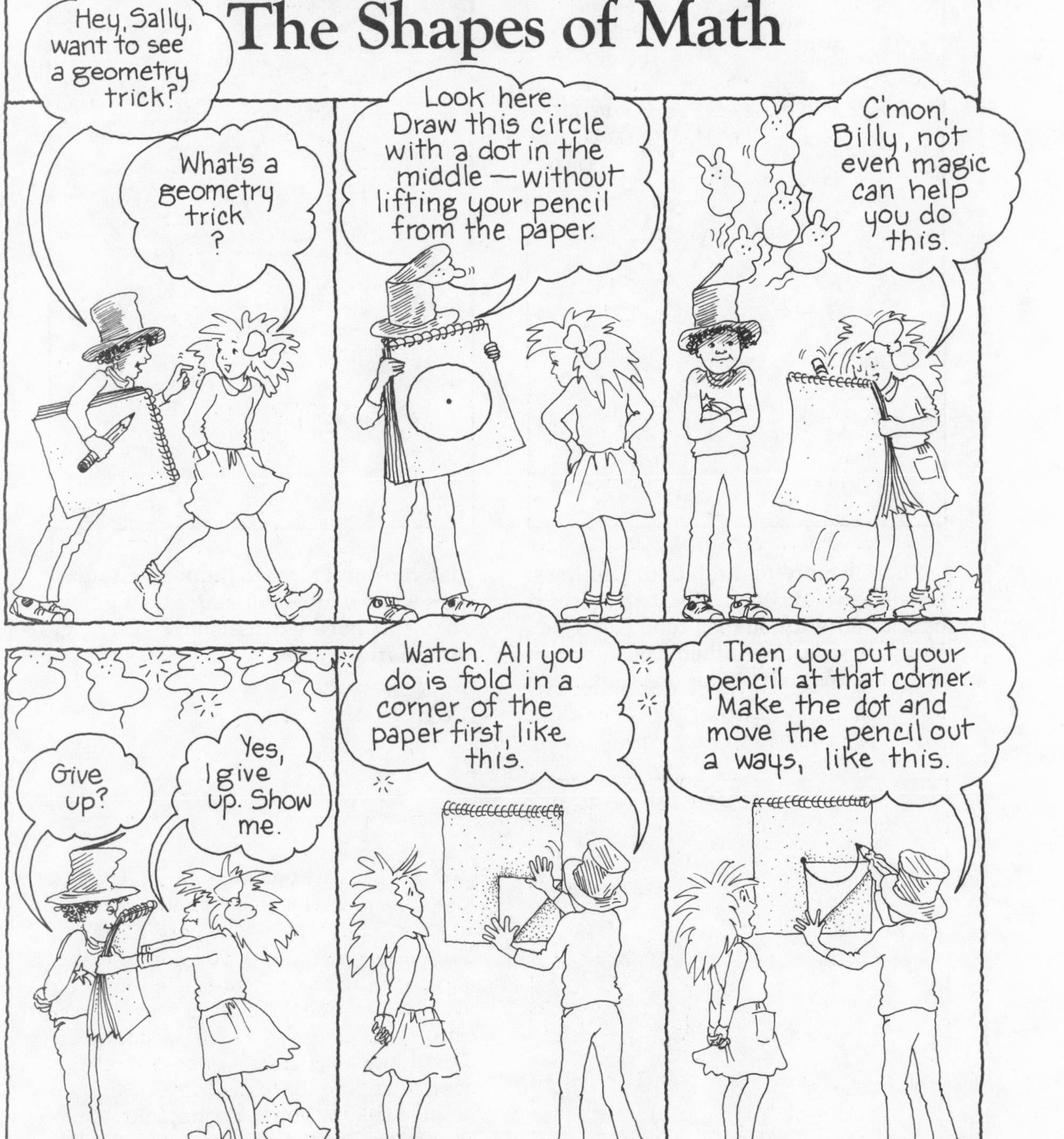

Hey, Sally, want to see a geometry trick?
What's a geometry trick?
Look here. Draw this circle with a dot in the middle — without lifting your pencil from the paper.
C'mon, Billy, not even magic can help you do this.
Give up?
Yes, I give up. Show me.
Watch. All you do is fold in a corner of the paper first, like this.
Then you put your pencil at that corner. Make the dot and move the pencil out a ways, like this.

There's more to math than numbers. Lots more. Mathematics has a great deal to do with shapes too. When you study shapes in mathematics, you're studying geometry. This does not mean that you don't have to think about numbers when you're thinking about geometry. But here it's the shape of things that matters most.

It Doesn't Always Look Simple

In mathematics a curve is any continuous line. It can have straight parts, angles, and curvy parts; but as long as you can draw it without lifting your pencil, it's called a curve.

If the curve doesn't ever cross over itself, it's a "simple" curve. If the curve ends up back where you started, it's called a "closed" curve.

There's more. There are simple closed curves. A simple closed curve is made when you get back to your starting place without ever crossing over the line at any point. If you have crossed over somewhere, then it's just a closed curve. It's enough to make you dizzy.

A circle is a simple closed curve. So is a triangle and a square and a pentagon and any polygon, for that matter. What's a polygon? Here we go again. A polygon is a shape made of straight line segments that connect and don't ever cross themselves.

That's enough for now. This stuff could make you crazy.

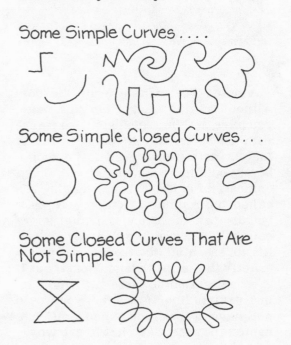

Some Simple Curves....

Some Simple Closed Curves...

Some Closed Curves That Are Not Simple...

Don't Make a Triangle

This is a two-person game of geometric strategy. You'll each need a pen or pencil— each of you must have a different color. First, trace the six dots as shown here for the playing board.

The way to play the game is to take turns drawing line segments. Each line segment connects two dots. The way to not lose is to avoid drawing three lines in your color that connect to make a triangle. If you do make a triangle in your color, you lose. The way to win is to force your opponent into having to draw a triangle in her color. If someone completes a triangle, but not all three sides are the same color, it doesn't count.

A note: To learn to draw the dots without tracing them from this page, you have to think "hexagon"—a figure with six sides. If you connect each of the six dots shown here to its neighbors, you'll have a hexagon with equal angles and sides of equal length. It's called a "regular hexagon," regular because all the sides and angles are equal. When drawing your own dots, it's not essential that they all be spaced exactly the same distance apart, but it is essential that no three of the dots lie in a straight line. If they did, you would not have a hexagon when you connected the dots. Sketch it to see why.

How many moves would this game take if you wound up connecting every dot with every other dot? How many line segments would that be? Connecting on the outside would give you the six line segments that make the hexagon. Connecting all those on the inside would give you lots more.

If you think that's too much drawing and counting, try thinking about the problem a different way. In mathematics it often helps to solve a problem by first solving a simpler one. Then you make the problem a little more complicated and solve that one. And as you keep doing this, you look for a pattern that will give you the answer to the hard problem, and perhaps to other related problems as well.

Instead of six dots, start with one dot. For one dot there aren't any lines you can draw. Pretty simple, huh?

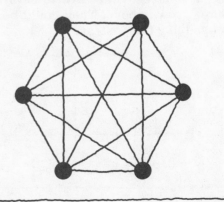

Okay, now move up to two dots. If you have two dots, there is only one possible line to draw.

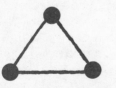

What about three dots? If you connect each of them, you have a triangle, and that's that.

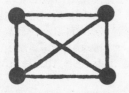

With four dots there are six lines.

Organizing this information makes it easier to examine.

DOTS	LINES
1	0
2	1
3	3
4	6
5	?

Continue the pattern, and use it to help you figure the answer for connecting five dots, six dots, or seven, or ten, or however many you'd like.

45

Geometry Joke

"Wanna hear a mathematical joke?"

"Yeah."

"Did you hear what the Mississippi acorn said when it grew up?"

"No, what?"

"Gee, Ah'm a tree."

"That's not even funny."

There's More Than One Way to Fold a Cube

If you cut this shape out of heavy paper or cardboard, you can fold it up and tape it into a cube.

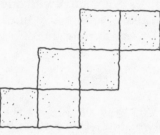

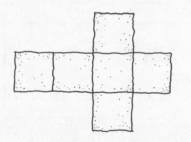

(Try it if you're not sure how it goes.)

Even though a cube has six sides and needs a shape with six squares to make it, the squares don't have to be in the shape shown above. They could be arranged like this instead:

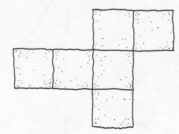

Besides these three arrangements, there are eight more ways to cut out six-square shapes that would fold up into cubes. You just need tape to hold them in shape. Try to find them.

Quick Change

Can you change a regular hexagon into a cube by drawing only three additional line segments?

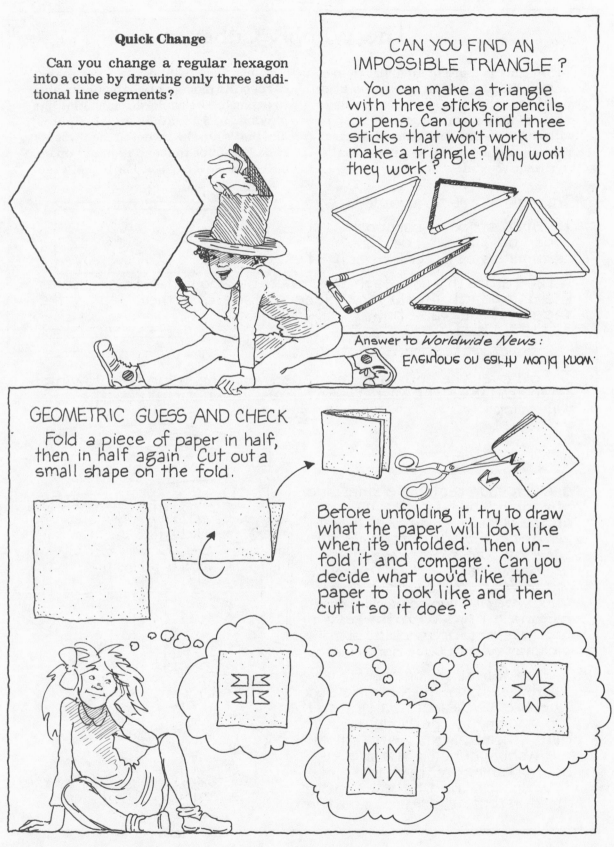

CAN YOU FIND AN IMPOSSIBLE TRIANGLE?

You can make a triangle with three sticks or pencils or pens. Can you find three sticks that won't work to make a triangle? Why won't they work?

Answer to *Worldwide News*:
Everyone on earth would know.

GEOMETRIC GUESS AND CHECK

Fold a piece of paper in half, then in half again. Cut out a small shape on the fold.

Before unfolding it, try to draw what the paper will look like when it's unfolded. Then unfold it and compare. Can you decide what you'd like the paper to look like and then cut it so it does?

The Wobbly Cube

Kim Hick is more of an artist than a mathematician, but he mixes both in his work, which is making stained-glass windows and mirrored shapes with intricate ins and outs of angles. Through his art he makes math that's terrific to look at.

In his work Kim Hick often makes cardboard models of shapes he wants to explore. The exploration is a lot like playing with mathematical figures, and that's how he invented the "wobbly cube," a shape that can lie flat, pop up, and take several shapes in between.

Try making one for yourself.

1. Cut 24 strips of cardboard 1 inch by 4 inches (or 2½ centimeters by 10 centimeters).

2. Lay 4 strips in a line, each separated by about the thickness of the cardboard. Run a long piece of tape over them, letting the tape overhang as shown.

3. Fold over the end with the tape overhang as in the drawing. Then fold over the other end. Press down firmly so the tape will stick.

4. Open your "rectangle ring" and reinforce it by taping each hinge on the outside. (*The best way to reinforce a hinge is to have the tape on both sides, directly opposite each other and touching in that little crack between the pieces.*) Then make five more rectangle rings with the rest of the strips. You should have six rings when you're done.

5. Tape four rings together from outside as shown. Then complete your wobbly cube by adding a ring to the top and one to the bottom.
Hint: There's always a way to hold the wobbly cube so the pieces you're taping will lie flat.
   When you have finished, explore the different shapes it can fold into.

Testing Your Geometry Memory

Remembering shapes in geometry isn't very hard for most people, except perhaps the stop-sign shape. Some people can't remember whether it has six sides or eight. (Do you remember?) Usually shapes are pretty easy.

Give yourself a quickie mental test. Can you picture a circle? A square? A pentagon? If you can, you're ready for the bigtime.

Remembering *sizes* in gemoetry is another story. Not so easy for some. See how you do.

Get a piece of paper and draw each of the following shapes as close to their actual sizes as you remember them. Then get out the objects and see how you did.

★ A **circle** the size of a U.S. quarter

★ A **rectangle** the size of a dollar bill

★ A **triangle** the size that a can opener makes in the top of a can

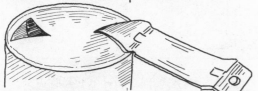

★ A **rectangle** the size of a standard playing card

★ A **square** the size of the end of a stick of butter

★ A **circle** the size of one of the holes on the telephone dial (or a **square** the size of one of the push buttons)

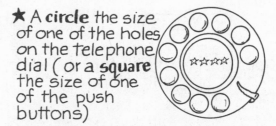

★ A **rectangle** the size of a stick of chewing gum

★ A **circle** the size of the buttons on your shirt or pants

Dinky buttons!

I was right!

How did you do? Try it again in a week or so to see if your memory improves. Is it important to remember sizes anyway?

Answer to *A Fraction Fooler*: The answer is one-half.

Answer to *Which Is Bigger?*: one quintillion or 10₁₈. They're both the same—

49

A GEOMETRY RIDDLE

With a geometric stretch of your imagination, can you explain how half of 8 might be 0 or 3?

Numbers Can Be Square

49

That probably happens when a pig eye is dividing up peanuts.

No!

Some numbers are square, and some aren't. If you want to test whether 9 is square, for example, you need to get nine objects. Pennies will work. You can line up nine pennies in rows so that each row has the same number of pennies in it, and together they make a square.

The number 8 isn't square. There's no way to push eight pennies into rows that make a square. It's no go. The number 4 works, however. Prove this to yourself. Then see if you can find other square numbers using this penny method. (You may even be able to talk your parents out of some spare, square change. Tell them there is a mathematical experiment in the works.)

To find square numbers you don't have to have pennies, or any objects at all; you can do it by multiplying. Pick any number and multiply it by itself. Let's take a small number, 3. Multiply 3 by 3 to get 9, which the penny test showed is a square number. Multiply 4 by 4 to get 16, another square number. Test that one with the pennies. Start even smaller, with a 1; 1 x 1 = 1, so 1 is a square number, even though one penny won't show it.

Oh brother, what a square!

17 × 17 = 289

49

Another nice thing about square numbers is that if you don't have pennies, and don't like to multiply either, you can find them by adding. Add up any string of odd numbers that are in order, starting with 1. For example, $1 + 3 + 5 = 9$, and you've already heard plenty about how square 9 is. Mathematicians say that any square number can be written as the sum of consecutive odd numbers.

Do you know how many squares there are on a checkerboard? There are 64—a square number, of course. Prove it by one of these methods. Then see if you can find the largest square number that is less than 1,000. (Your calculator may help here.)

$1 + 3 + 5 + 7 + 9 + 11 + 13 =$

Well, they *are* a little odd.

49

Strange Squares

Before you put away your calculator, look at this strange situation. Some pairs of square numbers have a peculiar characteristic. Take 144 and 441. They are the reverse of each other, right? To get 144, you can multiply 12 by 12; 441 is 21 times 21. And 12 and 21 are the reverse of each other as well!

This happens for 169 and 961 also.

$$13 \times 13 = 169$$
$$31 \times 31 = 961$$

It turns out that 12 and 13 are the only two-digit numbers that act this way. There are larger numbers that act like this, however.

$$112 \times 112 = 12,544$$
$$211 \times 211 = 44,521$$

Check this arithmetic with your calculator. Can you find any other squares that have this unusual trait?

144

441

Numbers Can Be Triangular Too

Numbers come in shapes other than squares. Some numbers are triangular. Get the pennies out again, and you can see why. You can arrange six pennies into a triangle, like this:

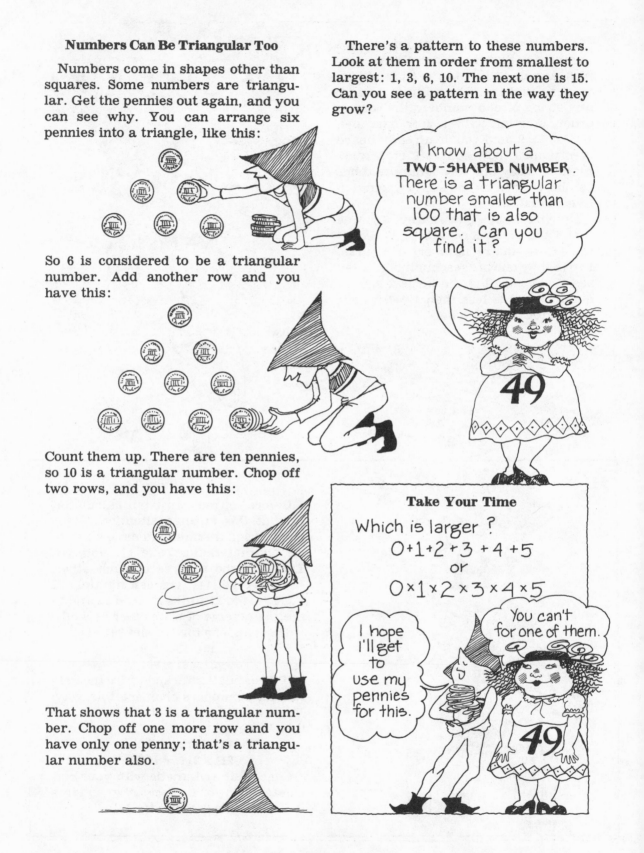

So 6 is considered to be a triangular number. Add another row and you have this:

Count them up. There are ten pennies, so 10 is a triangular number. Chop off two rows, and you have this:

That shows that 3 is a triangular number. Chop off one more row and you have only one penny; that's a triangular number also.

There's a pattern to these numbers. Look at them in order from smallest to largest: 1, 3, 6, 10. The next one is 15. Can you see a pattern in the way they grow?

I know about a **TWO-SHAPED NUMBER**. There is a triangular number smaller than 100 that is also square. Can you find it?

49

Take Your Time

Which is larger?
$$0 + 1 + 2 + 3 + 4 + 5$$
or
$$0 \times 1 \times 2 \times 3 \times 4 \times 5$$

I hope I'll get to use my pennies for this.

You can't for one of them.

49

52

Pictures of Math

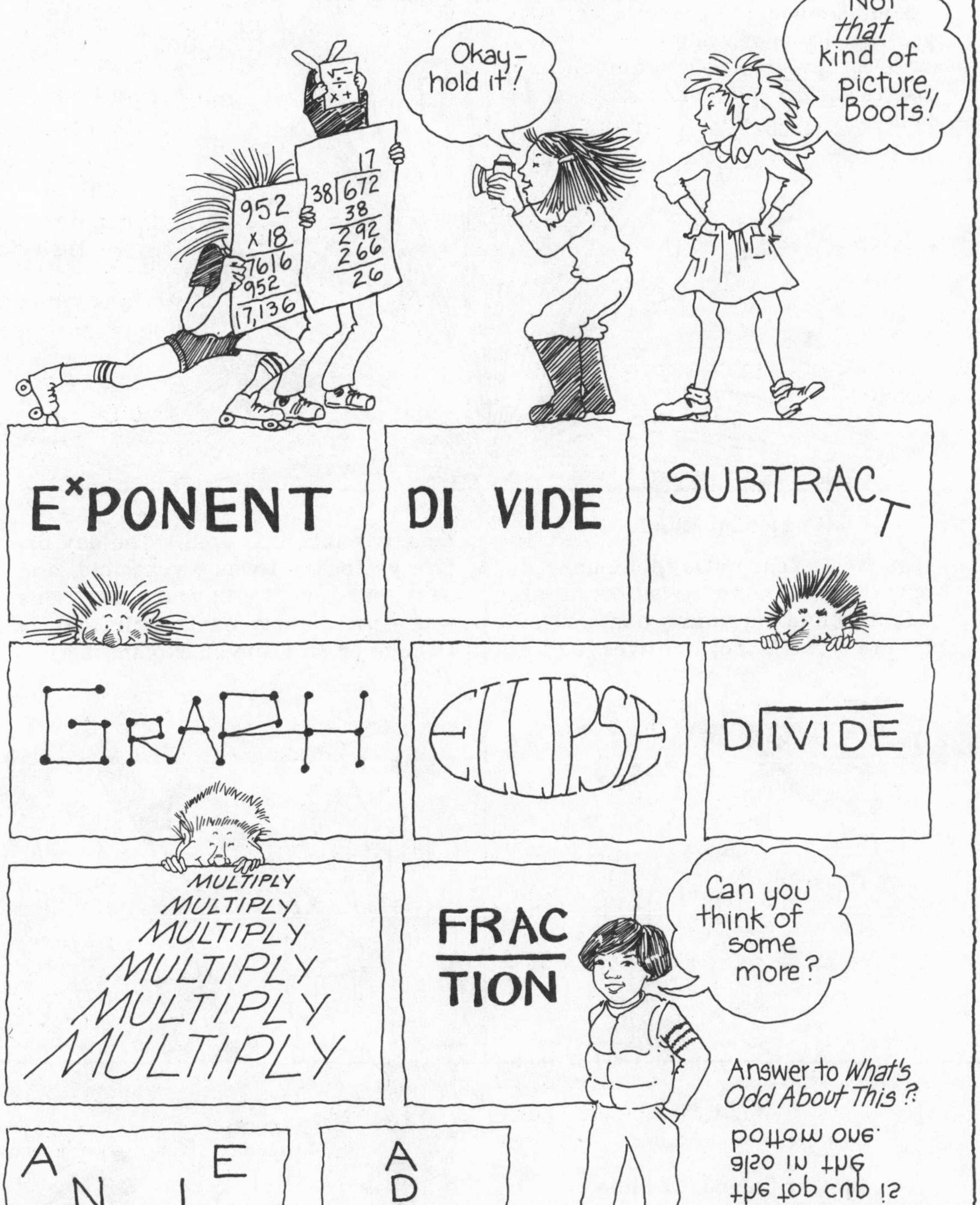
952
x 18
7616
952
17,136
17
38|672
38
292
266
26
Okay-hold it!
Not *that* kind of picture, Boots!
EXPONENT
DI VIDE
SUBTRACT
GRAPH
ELLIPSE
DIVIDE
MULTIPLY
MULTIPLY
MULTIPLY
MULTIPLY
MULTIPLY
MULTIPLY
FRAC
TION
Can you think of some more?
ANGLE
ADD
Answer to *What's Odd About This?*
Put one cup in another. Then whatever is in the top cup is also in the bottom one.

An Open Book

If you open this book so the two facing pages are numbered 40 and 41, the product of those two numbers is 1,640.

Just in case you've forgotten, the product is the answer to a multiplication problem.

Where do you need to open the book so that the product of the two facing page numbers is 12,656?

A Calendar Riddle

On New Year's Day, January 1, some relatives came to visit the family of a mathematical smarty pants. "How old are you?" the relatives asked.

SMACKO!

Smooch!

Smarty pants answered, "The day before yesterday I was 9 years old, and next year I will be 12 years old." This was true. Smarty pants's birthday is December 31. Can you explain this?

I thought you said she was smart.

Another Calendar Riddle

On what day will you celebrate having been alive for one billion seconds? How old will you be?

Can a person live that long?

I think we already have..

PART 3
Math for Two

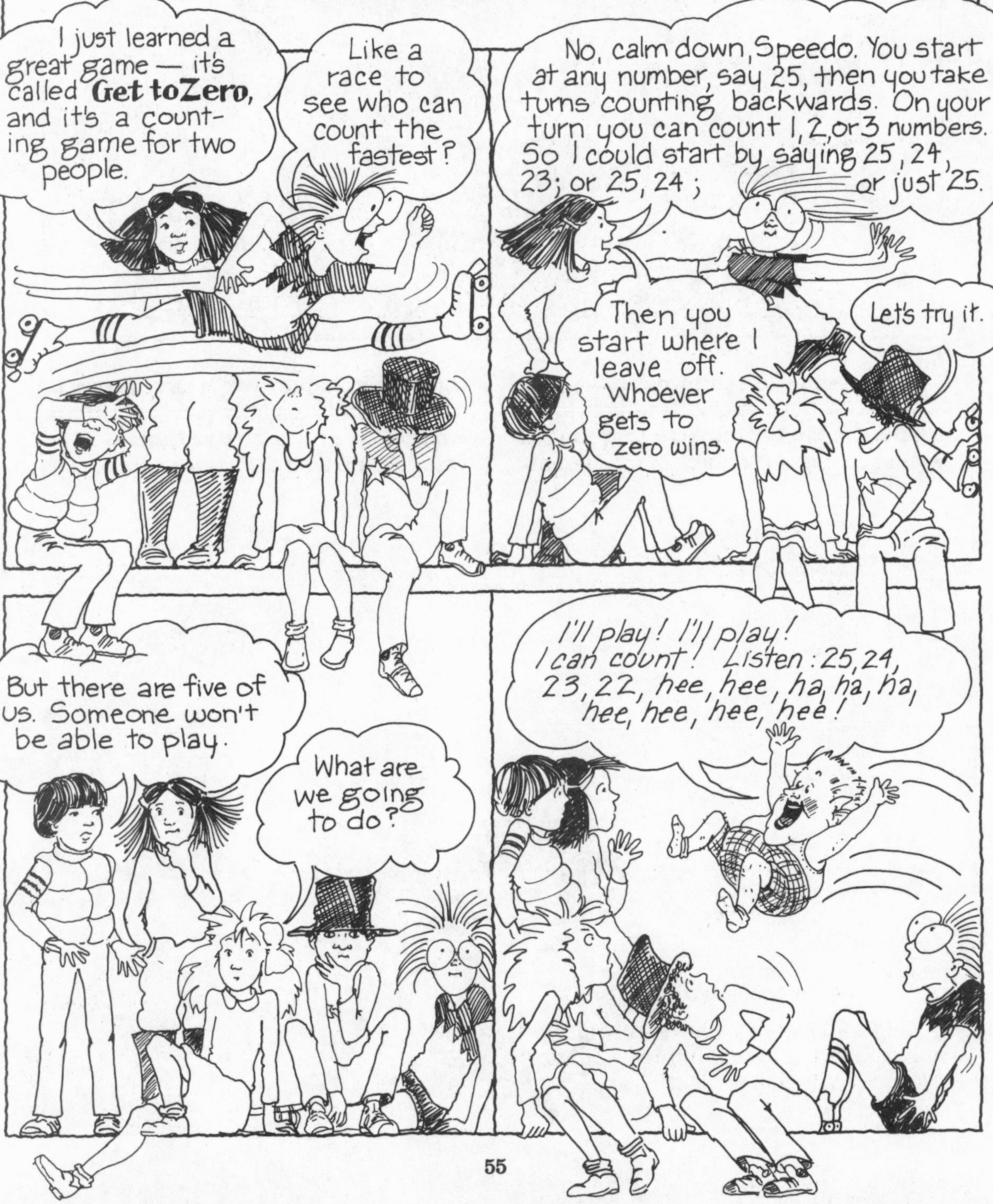
I just learned a great game — it's called **Get to Zero**, and it's a counting game for two people.
Like a race to see who can count the fastest?
No, calm down, Speedo. You start at any number, say 25, then you take turns counting backwards. On your turn you can count 1, 2, or 3 numbers. So I could start by saying 25, 24, 23; or 25, 24; or just 25.
Then you start where I leave off. Whoever gets to zero wins.
Let's try it.
But there are five of us. Someone won't be able to play.
What are we going to do?
I'll play! I'll play! I can count! Listen: 25, 24, 23, 22, hee, hee, ha, ha, ha, hee, hee, hee, hee!

It's possible to figure out a way to win Get to Zero every time you play. That's the kind of thinking that makes games a part of the study of mathematics. In this chapter you'll have plenty of opportunity to learn games, and mathematical ways to analyze them. Find yourself a friend and give them a go.

Games Mathematicians Play

Games that interest mathematicians have one thing in common—they require strategy. Games that have mathematical interest aren't the helter-skelter games in which luck is the major force. They're games where there is a plan for action, games where decisions about which moves to make depend on some rule. That rule is the strategy.

What mathematicians search for in games is the "winning strategy." A winning strategy is a rule for playing so you'll win no matter what your opponent does. Playing a game like this isn't very interesting once you know the winning strategy. (That's what mathematicians say, although some kids might argue.) Figuring out the winning strategy is the fun part.

Sometimes it's not possible to come up with a winning strategy for a game, but it is possible to come up with a strategy that guarantees you won't lose. This is called a "drawing strategy." Tic-tac-toe is an example. When two crackerjack tic-tac-toe players get together, their games usually end in a draw, a tie. That's because there is no winning strategy for that game. The best you can do is to make sure you do not lose.

57

Race for New Year's Eve

This is a calendar game, but you don't need a calendar to play it. What you do need is a friend.

The idea of this game is to be the first one to say "December 31." There are several rules you must follow as you take turns saying dates. Whatever date you say must be later in the year than the date said before it, and you may change only the month *or* the day, not both.

Suppose the person who is first starts by saying "February 2." The next has to say a later date. It could be a later day in February, February 10, for example, a change only of the day. Or it could be a later month, keeping the same day, such as "March 2" or "June 2." You can skip months or days, but you can change only the month *or* day, and your date must be later in the year than the one said before it.

You might be wondering what in the world this has to do with mathematics. First of all, it's a game of strategy, and that's enough to make it a respectable addition to any mathematics book. Also, there's a winning strategy for this game. With some mental sleuthing, you can figure out whether it's a good idea to go first and what are good moves.

One way to work out a strategy is to think backwards. For instance, if you say January 31 (or the 31st of any month), your opponent can automatically win by leaving the 31 the same and changing the month to December. That's a legal move. Or if you say any day (except the 31st) in December, you're also sunk. As a matter of fact, if your opponent says November 30, you can't win. Can you figure out why? Starting with the end of the game and thinking backwards can give you some valuable clues.

What would happen if there were three of you playing? Is it possible to figure a winning strategy for a three-person game of Race for New Year's Eve?

Twists on Tic-Tac-Toe

Tic-tac-toe is a game with some advantages. It can be played nearly everywhere, and it can be played in any weather. The only equipment it takes is some paper and a pencil, and the rules are easy to learn.

It has a disadvantage also. It gets boring pretty fast, but don't give up on tic-tac-toe yet. With a few changes, you can play some variations on the game that will challenge the best of players.

Your Choice Tic-Tac-Toe. Take turns as you usually do. On your turn you may put down either an X or an O, and you can change your mind from turn to turn. So can your opponent. The winner is the one who finishes any row, column, or diagonal of all X's or all O's.

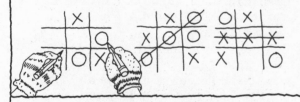

Number Tic-Tac-Toe. You don't use X's or O's for this version; you use the numbers from 1 to 9. Each number may be used only once in a game. Take turns writing a number in a space. The idea is to be the one to get the numbers in any row, column, or diagonal to add up to 15.

Last One Wins. The X's and O's don't matter so much in this game. The rule for play is this: On your turn, mark as many spaces as you like that are empty, as long as the ones you mark are all in the same row or column (not diagonal). Whoever fills in the last space is the winner.

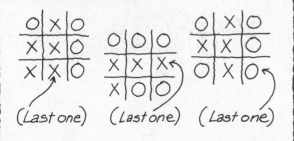

(Last one) (Last one) (Last one)

Tic-Tac-Toe for a Crowd. This game works well for from three to six people. You need a giant tic-tac-toe board to play on, one that is at least 10 by 10 instead of 3 by 3. Each of you chooses a different letter or mark or color crayon to use. The idea is the same as tic-tac-toe, except that instead of winning with three in a row, the winner has to get four in a row.

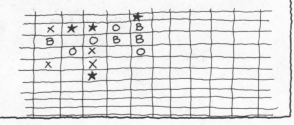

Keeping Track

Two kids were playing tic-tac-toe. The way they kept score was that at the end of each game the loser gave the winner a penny. When they stopped playing, one had won three games and the other had three more pennies than she started with. How many rounds had they played?

Having a Mathematical Conversation

You and a pal can see how sharp your mathematical conversation can be with this one. You need some objects to build with. They can be small blocks you have around the house — poker chips, dice, pencils, paper clips. It's essential that each of you has the same collection of stuff, exactly. Between six and ten objects will do.

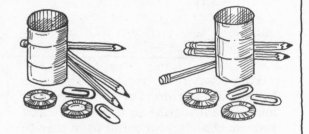

Now seat yourselves at a table and use a large box or cereal box to make a wall between you. The idea is that you can't see each other's working space.

One of you builds something with the objects. When you have built it, your job is to describe it well enough to the other person so that person can build exactly what you did. You can't see what your friend is building, and your friend can't see what you have built.

Your friend can ask questions, so it's a two-way conversation.

When you're both satisfied that you have done the best you can, lift the barrier and see how you did. Change roles and try again.

Which words helped and which did not? This game shows the need for good clear language and the ability to use that language well. How are you at mathematical talking?

Now, balance the third pencil on top of the can.

Bagels

Maybe you think bagels are something to eat. You're right. Maybe you also think that there has to be some reason, a really good one, for bagels to be included in a math book. Right again. And maybe you're thinking that including bagels in a math book probably has something to do with geometry, what with bagels being round and all. Well, you're wrong. In this math book, anyway, bagels have nothing to do with geometry, but everything to do with strategy.

"Bagels" is the name of a two-person game. It's a guessing game, but one that has a good deal of strategy to it. Each player thinks of a number; a three-digit number is good for starters. Take turns guessing each other's number. Whoever guesses the other person's number first wins.

Whenever one player makes a guess, the other gives some clues. Making good use of the clues is where the strategy comes in. There are three clues:

Pico means that one of the guessed digits is correct but is in the wrong place;
Fermi means that one of the guessed digits is correct and is also in the correct place;
Bagels (I'll bet you were wondering when the bagels part was coming in) means that none of the digits in the guess are correct.

If the guess contains more than one correct number, you give a combination clue such as **pico fermi** or **two fermi** or **two pico, one fermi**.

If Bagels whets your appetite for games, try it with four digits. Or more.

61

Guess My Word

Howdy! I'm **Weldon the Magic Bunny**, here to tell you about a two-person game that proves mathematics is everywhere, even in words. Here's how the game is played. One of the two of you thinks of a word — a three-letter word for starters. The other gets to guess it.

Box?
Nah.
Pie?
Nah.
Cap?
Nah.

Well, what is your word?

I keep telling you, it's "nah"!

Now that you've calmed down, we can continue with our rules. When one person makes a guess, the other has to tell whether the guess comes before or after the real word in the alphabet.

That way the game has some strategy to it, not just helter-skelter guessing. It's okay for the guesser to use paper and pencil to keep track of the guesses. Now try that one. And try to guess the other person's word in as few guesses as possible.

see?

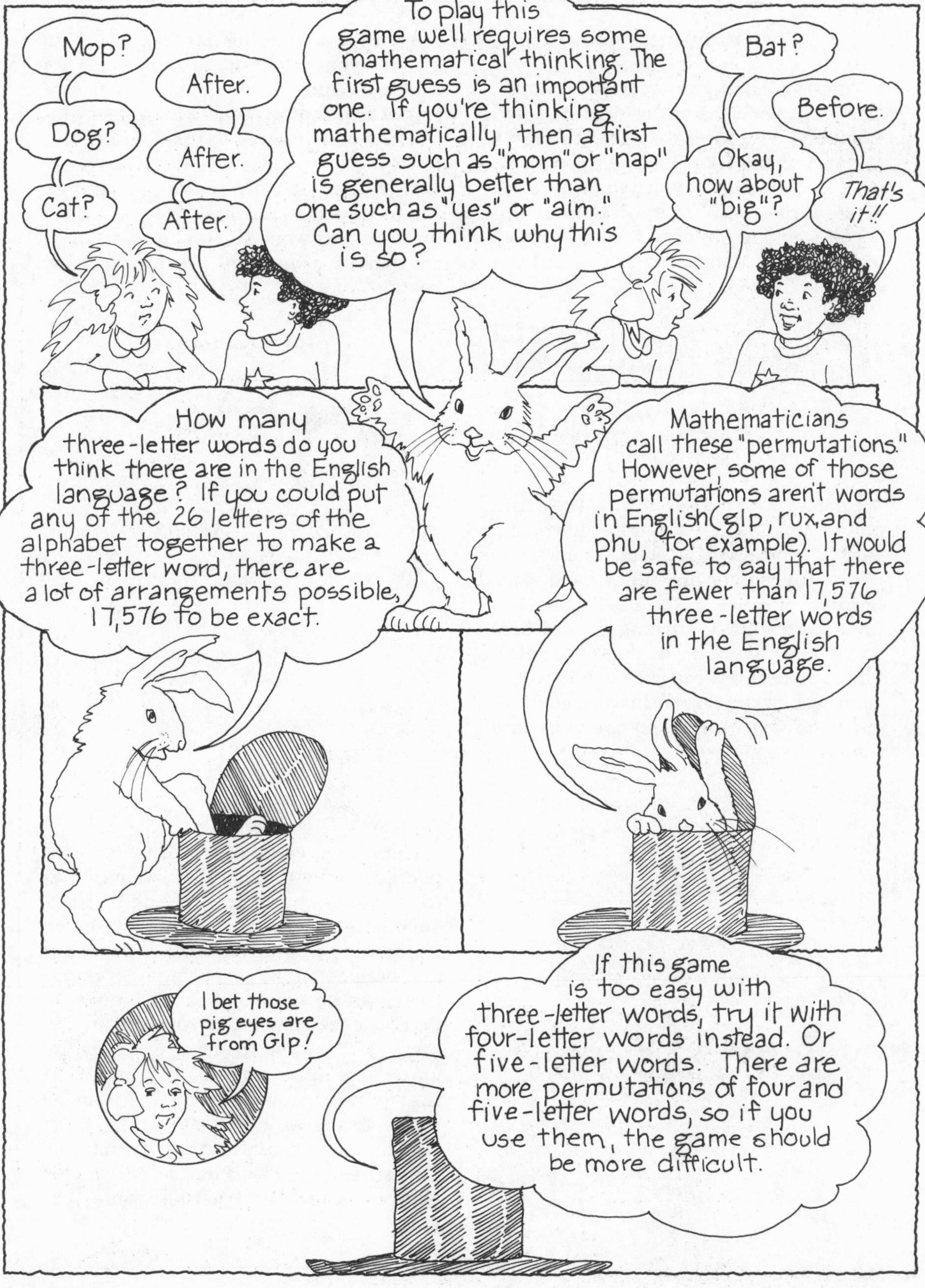
Mop?
Dog?
Cat?
After.
After.
After.
To play this game well requires some mathematical thinking. The first guess is an important one. If you're thinking mathematically, then a first guess such as "mom" or "nap" is generally better than one such as "yes" or "aim." Can you think why this is so?
Bat?
Okay, how about "big"?
Before.
That's it!!
How many three-letter words do you think there are in the English language? If you could put any of the 26 letters of the alphabet together to make a three-letter word, there are a lot of arrangements possible, 17,576 to be exact.
Mathematicians call these "permutations." However, some of those permutations aren't words in English (glp, rux, and phu, for example). It would be safe to say that there are fewer than 17,576 three-letter words in the English language.
I bet those pig eyes are from Glp!
If this game is too easy with three-letter words, try it with four-letter words instead. Or five-letter words. There are more permutations of four and five-letter words, so if you use them, the game should be more difficult.

The Thirty-one Game

This is a card game for two people. You don't need the entire deck to play. You need only 24 cards, ace through 6 of each of the four suits. If you don't have playing cards, you can make a set of 24 cards, with four of them numbered 1, four numbered 2, and so on up to four cards numbered 6. Lay out the 24 cards face up.

Decide who goes first. The first player turns any card face down and says that number out loud. The second player turns over any other card, adding that number to the first one. Continue taking turns turning a card face down and keeping a running total. Whoever reaches the sum of exactly 31 wins. If neither player hits 31, or if no one goes over 31, then no one wins that round.

There's a winning strategy to this game (you might have suspected as much). Which of you goes first is one important factor of the winning strategy, and which cards to turn over is the other.

If this game gets tiresome, change the total you're aiming for to 30, or 22, or 50. If you were to play for a total of 84, would you want to go first or second?

Race for Zero

Here is a calculator game for two people. You will need just one calculator. Whoever is first punches in a seven-digit number. The second player chooses one of the numerals showing and punches it in, repeating it as many times as he or she pleases, and subtracts it from what is already in the display. Then the first player takes the calculator again, chooses any numeral that is now showing, punches it in as many times as he or she likes, then subtracts it. Continue taking turns. The player who gets zero on the calculator display after subtracting wins the game.

PART 4

Logical Puzzles

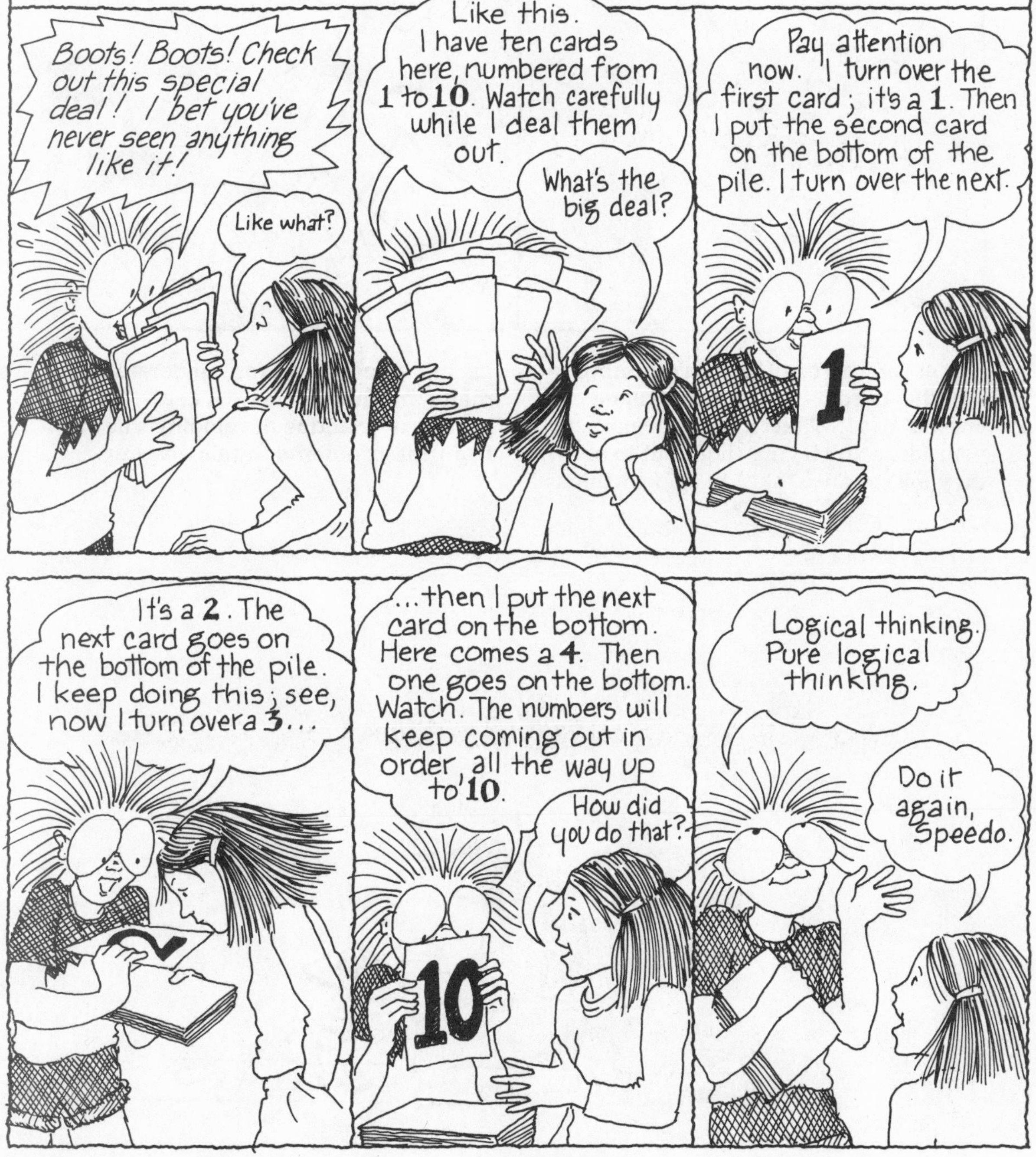
Boots! Boots! Check out this special deal! I bet you've never seen anything like it!
Like what?
Like this. I have ten cards here, numbered from 1 to 10. Watch carefully while I deal them out.
What's the big deal?
Pay attention now. I turn over the first card; it's a 1. Then I put the second card on the bottom of the pile. I turn over the next.
1
It's a 2. The next card goes on the bottom of the pile. I keep doing this; see, now I turn over a 3...
...then I put the next card on the bottom. Here comes a 4. Then one goes on the bottom. Watch. The numbers will keep coming out in order, all the way up to 10.
How did you do that?
10
Logical thinking. Pure logical thinking.
Do it again, Speedo.

You have to use logical reasoning to get the cards in order for Speedo's special deal. That means organizing your ideas and trying them out to see if they make sense. Skill in logical thinking is necessary for understanding many mathematical concepts. You'll get lots of practice developing this skill from the problems in this chapter.

A Special Deal

It's easy to make the equipment for the special deal that Speedo showed Boots. Use playing cards, or number ten index cards or pieces of paper. It's not so easy, however, to arrange the cards so you can deal them out as Speedo did. If you can get someone else interested in solving this problem, life might be simpler. People have devised different ways for figuring out how to arrange the cards, and two different points of view may be useful.

Once you figure it out, you should be able to arrange the pile for any number of cards and have the system work. If you're using playing cards, try it with ace through king. And if you're still interested, here are two more versions to tackle.

1. Put two cards on the bottom each time instead of one.

2. Try it with a spelling twist. Start by spelling out the number ("one"). When you say "o," put a card on the bottom. When you say "n," put another card on the bottom, and do the same for "e." Turn over the fourth card, and it should be the 1. Now for 2. Put three cards on the bottom, one at a time, spelling "two," then turn over the next; it should be a 2. Continue all the way to the end.

Answer to *An Open Book:*
The pages are 112 and 113.

★ $1 SENTENCE ★

Prevent Inflation.

The Pizza Problems

This is the only known collection of mathematical pizza problems. You may have thought there was no mathematics in pizza. Well, there is. It turns out there is mathematics in plain cheese pizzas, sausage pizzas, pepperoni pizzas, pineapple pizzas, teriyaki pizzas, and avocado pizzas, just to name a few. (Sometimes, it's just not good to take mathematics too seriously.)

Pizza Problem No. 1. **What time would it be if you gave one-eighth of a pizza to one friend and one-eighth of a pizza to another friend? Hint: Not only do you have to believe that mathematics can be silly at times, you have to add fractions to solve this one.**

Pizza Problem No. 2. **What looks exactly like half a pizza? Hint: This is another one that tests what you really know about fractions. The answer to this problem is not your neighbor's bulldog. You don't have to be told that wisecracks like that can hurt.**

Pizza Problem No. 3. Why did Mr. Fibonacci ask to have his large cheese, pepperoni, salami, onion pizza cut into six pieces instead of eight? Hint: Some of the information in this problem is there just to throw you off the track. The most important clue isn't even in the problem, and it is that Mr. Fibonacci really doesn't understand much about fractions. When asked, he was unable to solve either of the first two problems.

Pizza Problem No. 4. How can you cut a pizza into eight slices, all the same shape and size, with only three cuts? Hint: You have to be willing to think messy for this one.

Pizza Problem No. 5. The favorite pizzas of Alicia, Mike, Patrick, and Sarah are anchovy, mushroom, pepperoni, and sausage. No one's name starts with the same letter as his or her favorite pizza. Mike and Sarah absolutely cannot stand anchovies, much less an anchovy pizza. Alicia and Mike know for sure that they hate pepperoni. What is each person's favorite pizza? Hint: To keep track of the information in a logical problem like this, it can help to make a chart for recording what you know.

	ANCHOVY	MUSHROOM	PEPPERONI	SAUSAGE
ALICIA				
MIKE				
PATRICK				
SARAH				

Pizza Problem No. 6. Jennifer and Steven's parents were planning to go on their yearly vacation to Coco Palms. Usually an adult comes to the house and stays with the kids. This year Jennifer and Steven begged and begged to be allowed to stay home alone, without any sitter. They promised to keep the house clean, do all their homework, and eat regularly.

Their parents said they'd agree, but on one condition. The condition was that Jennifer and Steven had to figure out how many days their parents would be gone. If they could, it would be proof that they were clever enough to deal with any problem that might come along.

It wasn't just a wild guess they had to make, however. Jennifer and Steven's mom was a mathematician, and she gave them a pizza problem to solve that would also give them the correct answer to their problem.

"Every night while we're away," their mom explained, "you'll have to eat at the local pizza parlor. And every night you have to order a different combination pizza, choosing two different ingredients from the list on the menu. How many nights will you have to eat there to have tried every possible combination pizza, each with two ingredients?"

Jennifer and Steven went down to the pizza parlor and got a menu. It listed 15 choices of ingredients.

How many different combination pizzas are there if each is made with 2 ingredients? Hint: If you'd like to think this problem through as a mathematician might, start small. Start with just 2 ingredients, and work your way up to 15. With 2 ingredients, pepperoni and sausage, for instance, there is only one possible pizza. If you add a third ingredient, meatball, then there are three possibilities: pepperoni-sausage, pepperoni-meatball, or sausage-meatball. Add a fourth and see what happens.

If you'd like to write like a mathematician as well as think like one, make a table. It can help you see the pizza pattern.

INGREDIENTS	PIZZAS
2	1
3	3
4	?

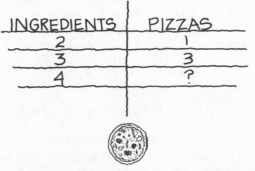

Pizza Problem No. 7. If it takes ten pizzamakers ten minutes to make ten pizzas, how long will it take five pizzamakers to make five pizzas?

Do you think they'll really be gone for three and a half months??

Good question. What's in Coco Palms, anyway?

September 4, 1974, was a great day in pizza history. At least it was in Little Rock, Arkansas. According to the Guinness Book of World Records, on that day the largest pizza was baked. It measured 25 feet 1 inch in diameter and weighed 1,200 pounds.

A Mathematical Tug-of-War

Your job in this mathematical contest is to decide who will win the final tug-of-war. The first two rounds give you the information you need.

The First Round. On one side there are four acrobats who have come down to the ground during the off-season for this special event. They have well-developed arm muscles because of all the swinging they do, and have proven themselves to be of equal strength. Remember that fact.

On the other side are five neighborhood grandmas, a tugging team that has practiced together for many, many years. They, too, are all equal in strength. Remember that fact also.

In the contest between these two teams, the result is dead even. Neither team can outtug the other. Remember that too.

The Second Round. One team is Ivan, the specially trained dog that got his start as a pup when he was taken out

for a walk by his owner. Ivan gets pitted against a team made up of two of the grandmas and one acrobat.

Again, it's a draw—an equal pull. Remember that fact.

It's the final tug that you must figure out. It will be between these two teams: Ivan and three of the grandmas on one side, the four acrobats on the other. Can you figure out who will win this tug-of-war?

One way to solve this problem is to use algebra, a branch of mathematics that uses equations to deal with relationships between quantities. If you haven't learned about algebra yet, you'll have to rely on logical reasoning. Either way it's mathematical thinking you must do. Get a pencil and paper to help you tug on this problem.

★ THE FINAL ROUND ★

Ice Cream and the Three Little Pig Eyes

Every afternoon the three little pig eyes take an ice cream break. They head to the closest ice cream store, where each orders a double-dip cone. There are only two different kinds of double dips that the pig eyes ever order. It's either a double-dip vanilla cone or a licorice-chocolate combination. (If you think that's weird, you haven't heard anything yet. Keep reading.)

If pig eyes #1 orders vanilla-vanilla, then pig eyes #2 orders the other. Either pig eyes #1 or pig eyes #3 orders vanilla-vanilla, but they never do so on the same day. Pig eyes #2 and pig eyes #3 never both order the licorice-chocolate combination on the same day.

Which of the three little pig eyes ate a vanilla-vanilla cone yesterday and will order a licorice-chocolate cone today?

Would you like a **hint**? Two of the three pig eyes always order the same cone — every day! It may be easier to figure out who those are, then you'll know who's left to fill the answer slot.
Want another **hint**? A chart may help.

Are you wondering who in the world the little pig eyes are? See page 22.

	Yesterday	Today
#1		
#2		
#3		

Who's Who?

Rachel, Mark, Joshua, and Maria are 9, 10, 11, and 13 years old. Joshua is older than Maria and younger than Rachel. Mark is younger than Joshua and older than Maria. How old is each? Hint: A chart can help.

	9	10	11	13
RACHEL				
MARK				
JOSHUA				
MARIA				

Deal and Count

This is a solitaire card game that is easy to play, yet not so easy to understand mathematically. The easy part first: Shuffle a deck of cards. Then deal them out, one by one. While you're dealing, count: ace, 2, 3, 4, 5, 6, 7, 8, 9, 10, jack, queen, king, ace, 2, 3, 4, and so on. Each time you deal a card, turn it over so you can see what it is. You win this game of solitaire if you get to the end of a deck without turning over a card that matches what you count.

Get It?

There's no skill to this game, no strategy. However the cards get shuffled determines the results. It's pure chance. But pure chance is something that interests mathematicians very much. To study pure chance is to study the part of mathematics called "probability."

In this game your chance of winning, and getting to the end of the deck with no match, isn't too terrific—a little more than 1/3. That's less than a 50-50 chance of winning. Not very hopeful. It doesn't mean that you'll win one out of every three games. Mathematical probability doesn't make promises like that. A probability of 1/3 means that, if you play many, many games, the more you play, the closer your number of wins will be to exactly 1/3 of all the games you play.

Play Deal and Count a bunch of times and keep track of your number of wins and number of games. Don't get frustrated when you lose—you're a mathematician, remember?

King Arthur's Problem

King Arthur had a problem. His daughter, Glissanda, loved mathematics so much that she spent most of her time solving problems, making geometric designs, and playing with numbers. That wasn't King Arthur's problem; he was proud of his daughter and her mathematical interest. Glissanda had reached the age when a young woman was permitted to marry, and she was definitely interested in marrying. In fact, she had one requirement for a husband: he must love mathematics (or at least like it a lot). For her, a life of evenings in front of a warm fire solving mathematical puzzles seemed like a sure way to marital bliss. Finding that mathematics-loving husband was King Arthur's problem.

Now, if this story had taken place in modern times, King Arthur wouldn't have had this problem. Glissanda would probably have met someone in her math classes who would be a fine mate, and that would be that. But in the days of King Arthur and his Knights of the Round Table, women didn't have much freedom; their husbands were chosen by their parents.

Now King Arthur loved Glissanda dearly, and he would do anything for his daughter, but he was confused about how to find a husband to suit Glissanda. After all, the Knights of the Round Table—they were the best men in the land—were outdoor types who spent their time bravely scouting the countryside for dragons to slay. He couldn't remember any of them ever even mentioning mathematics.

King Arthur was perplexed. He thought about it for days. And days stretched into weeks, but no ideas came to him.

Meanwhile he had his kingly work to do, but he became so distracted by this marriage problem that he couldn't concentrate. King Arthur was definitely not himself. One morning at the meeting he was very short-tempered with his knights. Little things seemed to bother him. At one point he even shouted out, "Can't you control that constant clanking of your armor and sit still?" The knights knew he must have something important on his mind.

That night at dinner King Arthur talked to Glissanda about the situation. "How shall I find out who is the cleverest in mathematics?" he asked her. "Should I just ask?"

"No, no," protested Glissanda. "That wouldn't be a good way. Some would answer yes just to become next in line to be king. I could get stuck with a husband who wants to do nothing at night except drink ale, one with no true interest in mathematical conversation. You must devise a mathematical test."

"What sort of test?" King Arthur asked.

"Let me think about it," Glissanda answered, wandering off, already deep in thought.

The next morning at breakfast Glissanda seemed cheerful.

"Do you have the test?" her father asked.

"Not yet," Glissanda answered, "but I'm working on it. Tell me, father, how many knights are there at your Round Table?"

"Well, that varies," he replied. "It depends on how many are back from a journey. Sometimes as many as 50, and sometimes only a handful. Why?"

But Glissanda didn't answer. King Arthur could tell she was lost in thought, with that glaze over her eyes that told him she was thinking about mathematics again. It made him think that her husband would need to be very understanding.

That night at dinner Glissanda made an announcement. "I've got the test," she said. "You can give it at your meeting tomorrow to the Knights of the Round Table."

King Arthur's face broke into a relieved smile. "Wonderful, wonderful!" he exclaimed. "But what if all the knights aren't present tomorrow? You know, I never can tell who will come."

"I've thought of that," Glissanda said. "In this test there is just one problem. Give it tomorrow to the knights who are present and announce that those interested in answering should reappear in one month's time with their solutions. In the meanwhile, they should spread the problem throughout the kingdom, so others who are off doing what knights do can come with solutions as well."

"What is the problem?" King Arthur asked eagerly.

Glissanda explained, "Suppose 24 knights came to a meeting of the Round Table. And suppose the 24 chairs were numbered in order, so that everyone knew which chair was number 1, and in which direction you will count to 24. In order to choose my husband, you draw your sword, point to the knight in the first chair, and say, 'You live.' Then point to the knight in chair number 2, say, 'You die,' and chop off his head. To the third knight you say, 'You live.' And to the fourth, you say, 'You die,' and chop off his head. You continue doing this around and around the circle, chopping off the head of every other living knight until just one is left. That's the one I'll marry."

Glissanda stopped talking.

"That's it?" her father asked, horrified. "You expect me to kill all of my knights but one? What kind of kingdom would I have then? There would be just you, your husband, a roomful of dead knights, and the rest of my knights cowering in the countryside for fear of ever returning to the Round Table. Is this what you call mathematics? Have you gone crazy?" King Arthur was shouting now. He couldn't believe his ears. He wanted Glissanda to be happy, but this was ridiculous.

"Oh, father," Glissanda said. "I wouldn't expect you to actually kill anyone. It's just a problem, and it definitely is mathematical. Besides," she went on, giggling a bit, "if you don't tell them you really won't chop heads, then only the brave knights will come. Then I'm sure to have a husband with courage as well as one with mathematical intelligence."

"But Glissanda," King Arthur went on, still rather upset, "I admit it's an unusual problem that is a true test of logical thought. But how do you know 24 knights will return that day to find the solution?"

Glissanda giggled a bit more, feeling even merrier. "That's the real point to the problem," she said. "Don't tell, but the knight of my dreams would know that he has solved the problem only if he knows where to sit for *any* number of chairs. I've been working on this problem, and there's a marvelous pattern for the solution!"

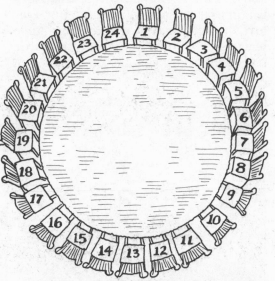

Which seat is the right one when there are 24 knights at the Round Table? Can you find the pattern for predicting which is the right seat for any number of chairs?

Logical Breakfast

The three little pig eyes have different ideas about what to eat for breakfast. Actually they have different ideas about almost everything, but this story is about breakfast. One of the pig eyes loves to eat granola with orange juice poured over it. Another of the little tricksters likes scrambled eggs with ketchup. The other likes to have a banana split, claiming that it helps one keep a sharp eye out for the unusual in life.

Your job, and it's a mathematical one, of course, is to find out which of the little pig eyes eats the banana splits for breakfast. To find out, you have to use some logical reasoning; it's difficult to tell just by looking at them.

(GARURP!)

Some **clues** about the lineup.
* Pig eyes #1 does not eat scrambled eggs with ketchup or banana splits.
* Pig eyes #2 does not eat scrambled eggs with ketchup. Those are all the clues you get. The rest is up to you.

Answer to *Take Your Time*:

Adding the numbers from 0 to 5 will be larger since 0 times anything is 0.

80

What's a Paradox?

Every once in a while mathematics runs into a kind of snag called a "paradox." This happens when something seems to make sense, and at the same time it seems impossible for it to make sense. A paradox is a contradiction and can make the best of mathematicians sit up and take notice.

There are different kinds of paradoxes. One is where something seems rather incredible, but because it can be proved to you, you have to accept it, even if it drives your imagination nuts. Optical illusions can be like that. Which of the two pencils is longer? Measure them to find out for sure.

An Infinite Paradox. In another kind of paradox, a contradiction appears because you've reasoned incorrectly about something. Most people think that a whole thing is always greater than any of its parts. That's true for an apple or a chocolate cake or anything you can hold and touch. But it's not always so in mathematics. Ideas can't always be held or touched and have to be examined in your mind.

Here's an example. Take all the counting numbers—1, 2, 3, 4, and so on. There are more of them than anyone can count, because no matter how far you go, you can always count one more. And then one more. And then one more, and so on. That's why mathematicians say that the set of counting numbers is infinite.

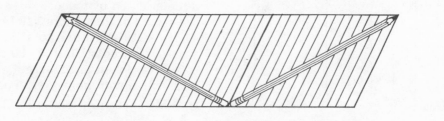

Now think about part of that set of counting numbers, just the odd numbers—1, 3, 5, 7, and so on. Since you skip every other one, you may think that there are half as many odd numbers as there are counting numbers. That may seem like a reasonable way to think, but it's wrong. That set of odd numbers is also infinite. It goes on and on forever.

You can't say that one infinite set is larger than another infinite set, since neither set will ever run out. (Weird things happen in the world of the infinite!) Incorrect reasoning can lead you to say something is true when it isn't, and there you are in the middle of a paradox.

The Line Paradox. There are many examples of paradoxes from incorrect reasoning in geometry. The line paradox is one that is centuries old. Trace the figure below onto a piece of paper so you can cut it out.

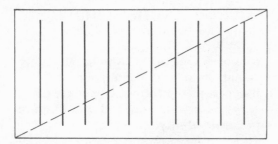

Count the lines inside the rectangle to make sure you believe there are ten of them. Now cut the rectangle along the dotted line, and slide the lower piece down and to the left, to the position shown below.

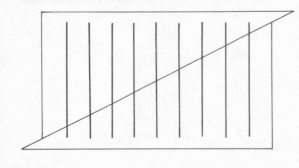

Count the lines inside the figure now. There are only nine! How did a line vanish? If you slide the lower part back, the missing line reappears. But where did it come from?

What happens is that no single line vanishes. Because of the way the rectangle is cut, 8 of the original 10 lines were cut into 2 pieces. Then there were 18 pieces of lines (count them in the original drawing to be sure you understand this), which got rearranged into 9 lines. Each of those 9 lines is longer than each of the original 10 lines were. There's still as much total line; it has just gotten redistributed. To think that a line vanished is incorrect reasoning and will never help you figure out a paradox.

The same idea has been used to make this puzzle. Trace these faces onto a piece of paper, cut on the dotted line, and slide the lower piece to the left. It will seem as if a face has disappeared! Can you explain this?

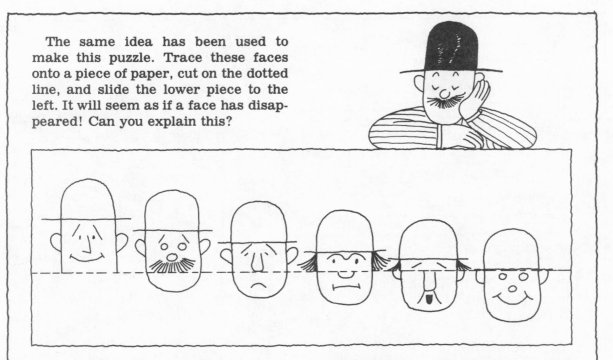

The Checkerboard Paradox. This is another geometric paradox, but this time an extra square seems to appear, rather than vanish. You start with an 8 by 8 square, ruled off into 64 squares, just like a checkerboard. Draw the lines inside as shown, label the pieces, then cut carefully on the lines drawn.

Rearrange the four pieces into a rectangle as shown.

Now you have a rectangle with 65 squares! See if you can figure out how to explain this paradox.

There is still another type of paradox —the logical paradox. This type can get quite complicated. Some of them have caused such confusion among mathematicians that, for some, explanations have not yet been found. Following are two for you to unravel.

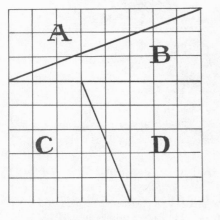

$$8 \times 8 = 64$$

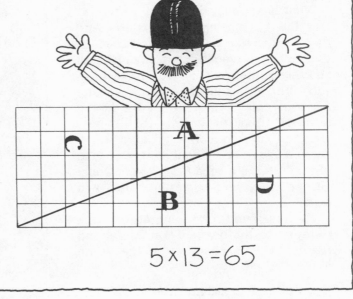

$$5 \times 13 = 65$$

The Barber Paradox. The only barber in a small village had a sign in his window.

This barber shaves everyone in the village who does not shave himself. No exceptions.

The sign caught the eye of a mathematician passing by. Actually it was the "No exceptions" that she noticed. This mathematician believed that every rule probably has exceptions.

What she wondered about was this: Did the barber shave himself? And that's when the paradox appeared. If the barber shaved himself, then he was shaving someone who did shave himself—himself—and that was breaking his own rule. But if he didn't shave himself, then, according to his own sign, he had to come to him to be shaved, since he shaved everyone who did not shave himself. No exceptions. Either way, he contradicts his own sign.

The mathematician pointed out this paradox to the barber. As the legend has it, he was never quite the same again.

One Last Paradox. If you can stand it, give this last one a try. Read it carefully first.

> 1. *This book has 300 pages.*
> 2. *The author of this book is Regina Carter.*
> 3. *The statements numbered 1, 2, and 3 are all false.*

For sure number 1 is false. (You can count for yourself if you don't believe the page numbers.) And for sure number 2 is false. Regina Carter has always hated mathematics, and probably always will, and would never be caught fooling around with math books (or paradoxes). But what about number 3? If it's true that statement 3 is false, then shouldn't 1 and 2 really be true, and how can something be both true and false at the same time? That's a paradox, which may be the only thing you're sure of now.

Want to know what I think about paradoxes? It would be a great name for a rock group — **The Paradoxes**. It fits perfectly. A rock group is supposed to play music, right? Well, for *my* ear, what they play is noise, garbage, not music. There's a contradiction for you. Yep, **The Paradoxes** would make it big, I bet.

Paradoxes in mathematics are not useless and silly tricks. They may be worth a laugh, or at least one hah, but that's not where their true worth lies. Paradoxes make you think about ideas and make you question what seems — but maybe it isn't — right. That kind of thinking is useful for many things, not only mathematics.

The Möbius strip I'm standing on on page 81 is a paradox. Paper has two sides, right? How many sides does a Möbius strip have?

Some people think that the strangest paradox of all is that there can be paradoxes in mathematics. They think that mathematics ought to be above that sort of perplexing thinking. It's not so, though. The Greeks first explored paradoxes, and even today new ones are being discovered. If you're interested in them, you may have a mathematical career cut out for you.

Is there a paradox lurking in this $1 sentence?

★ $1 SENTENCE ★

Surely highways prevent problems.

What's Odd About This?

If you try this problem at the dinner table, you might get your parents so interested that they will forget you haven't eaten your broccoli. But then again, you might not. In either case there's some mathematics here worth trying.

For this problem you need three cups and 11 objects. Coins or paper clips will work—any objects that will fit inside the cups. Here's the problem. Put the 11 objects into the three cups so that there are an odd number of objects in each cup. How many ways can you do it so that each arrangement is different?

That problem shouldn't give you much trouble. But before you put away the cups and objects and get back to your broccoli, try this one. Get rid of one of the objects, so you have three cups and ten objects. Now try the same problem, still trying to put an odd number of objects in each cup. This time, it's not so obvious. It can be done, but there's a trick to it. Using the trick, one person claims there are 10 different ways. Another claim is 15 different ways, using another trick.

Since a trick is needed here, and that doesn't seem quite mathematically fair, here's a hint: Can you find a way for an object to be in two cups at the same time?

In case the hint doesn't help and you're going nuts, there is one solution to this problem in the book. Finding it is up to you, though. (We can't tell everything!)

PART 5
Statistical Stuff

Statistics are important for lots of people—toy manufacturers, for example, who need to learn what kinds of toys and games will appeal to kids; policemen who need to know about traffic patterns in order to decide where new lights or stop signs are needed; television producers who need to know what kinds of television shows will have appeal; newscasters who want to know about the popularity of candidates during elections; shoe-store owners who need to know how many of each shoe size to stock; and on and on. Collecting and analyzing statistics is an important part of mathematics. Here's your chance to learn about statistics, and even to collect some yourself.

The Mathematics of a Pencil

Every year Americans buy approximately 2½ billion pencils, the regular kind that is usually yellow and needs sharpening from time to time. That's a lot of pencils—an average of one each month for every person.

The kind of pencil you use today, with a round lead inside, was invented over 100 years ago, in 1879. Before then the lead in pencils was square and not so easy to use. Actually it's not correct to say the lead is either round or square since it really isn't "lead" at all. It's a mixture of graphite and clay; lead never was used in pencils. But graphite used to be called "black lead," so that's probably why we still refer to it as lead.

Getting all the ingredients for making a batch of pencils is a task of worldwide proportions. The wood comes from cedar trees on the Pacific Coast of the United States. Clay comes from the state of Georgia. Graphite comes from Madagascar. Also used are wax from the carnauba palm tree of Brazil and a gum called "tragacanth" from the Middle East.

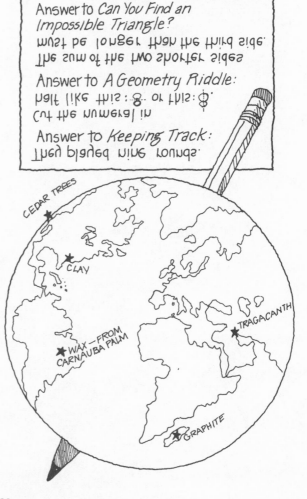

Answer to *Can You Find an Impossible Triangle?*
The sum of the two shorter sides must be longer than the third side.

Answer to *A Geometry Riddle:*
Cut the numerals in half like this: 8. or this:

Answer to *Keeping Track:*
They played nine rounds.

Perhaps this doesn't sound like stuff for a book on mathematics. It seems to belong in a history book or a geography book. So let's get to the mathematics part—statistics. Pencil statistics.

If you laid a year's supply of pencils end to end, they would circle the earth 5 times.

One pencil can be sharpened approximately 17 times.

One pencil can be used to write about 45,000 words.

Now, Suzanne, write "I will not throw pencils in class" until you have used up that brand new pencil.

One pencil can draw a line about 33½ miles long (56 kilometers, if you're thinking metric).

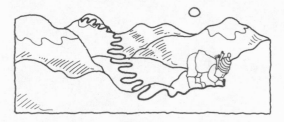

That means a year's supply could trace the distance to the moon and back about 200,000 times.

You should be able to make about 4,000 checkmarks with a pencil before you absolutely must sharpen it.

America's 100 billionth pencil was manufactured in 1976 and was displayed at the Smithsonian Institute.

Had enough? If not, see if you can find out what it means when a pencil is a number 2, or 2½, or 1, or 3. Now warm up your calculator. If the same number of pencils continued to be made each year (2½ billion), in what year will the quintillionth be made? Or the nonillionth? Or the tredecillionth? (Check page 121 if you have no idea what these words of enormity mean.)

★$1 SENTENCE★

Writing upsets Suzanne.

Food Statistics

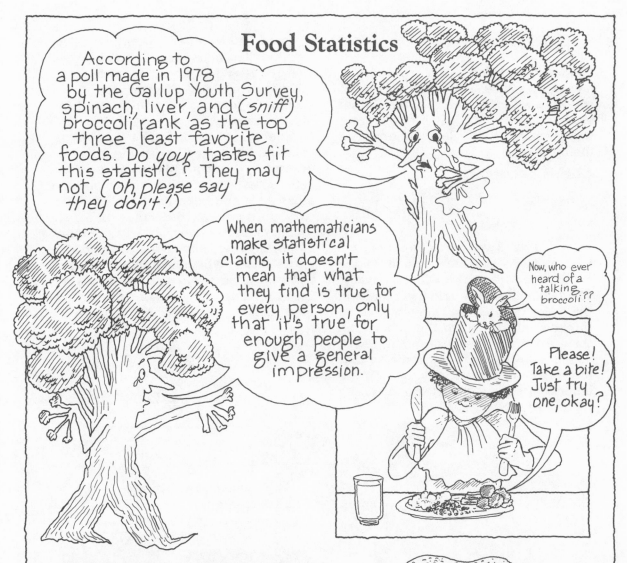

You have to look at statistics with a sharp eye. They can be misleading. Though the poll revealed that spinach was the least favorite food of kids, it was 20 percent of the kids asked who reported that their least favorite food was spinach. That's only one out of every five kids asked! It's true that spinach led the list of least favorites, but it wasn't even the opinion of half the kids asked. With liver, 19 percent of the kids polled gave it as their least favorite. And 8 percent named broccoli. Other kids gave different choices: vegetables in general, beans, peas, and fish.

When kids were asked about their favorite foods, the top four winners were Italian food, steak, hamburgers, and chicken or turkey. Other favorites listed included seafood, vegetables, potatoes, Mexican food, and fish. (Notice that vegetables and fish made both the favorite and the least favorite categories. There is no pleasing everyone when it comes to taste.)

91

Be a Pollster

How about taking your own survey and seeing how the results you get compare with the results of the Gallup survey? There are several different ways you can do it. See which makes the most sense to you.

Food Poll Number 1. Prepare two lists of foods that correspond to the foods reported on the Gallup survey. The two lists shown below list foods in the order that the poll produced. You might want to mix up the order, and then, after your results are in, see if your final ranking is the same as that of the Gallup results. You'll need another copy of each list on which to tally the response you get.

Food Poll Number 2. Don't have lists for kids to choose from. Just ask two questions: What is your favorite food? What is your least favorite food? Then compare your results with those of the Gallup survey.

There are other things you might also be interested in finding out. For example, do girls and boys have different tastes? The Gallup survey showed that girls and boys have tastes which are pretty much the same, but girls seem to dislike liver and spinach more than boys do, and like Italian food a little better. What about adults' tastes? Are they the same as kids' tastes, or are they different? Make a prediction, then poll some adults and compare.

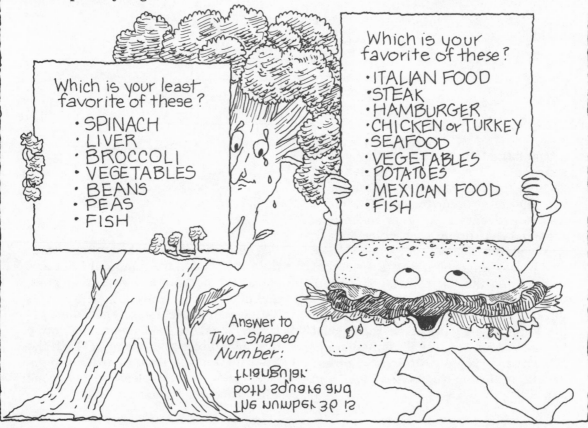

Which is your least favorite of these?
- SPINACH
- LIVER
- BROCCOLI
- VEGETABLES
- BEANS
- PEAS
- FISH

Which is your favorite of these?
- ITALIAN FOOD
- STEAK
- HAMBURGER
- CHICKEN or TURKEY
- SEAFOOD
- VEGETABLES
- POTATOES
- MEXICAN FOOD
- FISH

Answer to Two-Shaped Number:

The number 96 is the same both rightside up and upside down.

The Mathematics of Polls

Taking polls that produce valid results deals with the branch of mathematics called "statistics." There really is no way to find out absolutely what is the least or most favorite food of kids; you can't possibly ask every kid in the world. The results of surveys and polls are based on asking just a part of the entire population, a "sample," it's called. How large a sample is an important factor when reporting reliable and believable results. The size of a sample may depend on the purpose of the poll.

Suppose you're polling kids' food preferences. How many kids you ask is important. If you're planning to invite six friends for a party, you may be able to ask all of them what they like to eat. That would be a poll of the entire population of party guests and would certainly be a sound statistical survey for your purpose. Planning your menu around what only one kid said is not as sensible. Polling five may do fine. But if you polled those six kids, then used that information to give a general report about which foods kids in the United States like and dislike, your results wouldn't be worth much statistically. So sample size is important.

Another consideration is where you get your sample. If you found that half or more of the kids you surveyed named Mexican food as their favorite, it may be true only where you live. There are some parts of the country where tacos and other Mexican food aren't popular, or even available. Some kids may love grits or pot stickers; others may never have tasted them. The makeup of your sample is an important factor in what results you report.

As you study more mathematics, you'll have the chance to learn more about statistics and how they're used. Getting some experience now can come in handy later.

93

In mathematics, 3! is a special number. It's not excited. That's not what the exclamation point is about. The exclamation point tells you that 3! is equal to 6. Well, that's what it tells mathematicians. Confused? You deserve an explanation. There's no room for confusion in mathematical thought. Things are tough enough without confusion.

The language first. How do you say "3!" out loud? You don't shout it. You say "three factorial." In mathematics the "!" stands for "factorial." That doesn't tell you much, but at least it's a start. Someone came along with a name for this funny creature, 3!, before you or I did, and we all go along with it.

The meaning second. Suppose you and two friends go into an ice cream store for cones. "Who's first?" the person behind the counter might ask. And when the first kid has received a cone, the person would most likely ask, "Who's next?" Well, how many different possibilities are there for you and your friends to be first, second, and third? The answer to that is 6—see if you can prove that to yourself before going on any farther. Then come back and continue reading.

Ready? The reason that 3! is equal to 6 is that if there are three of you in line for ice cream cones, then there are six different ways you could line up.

Oh no.

Suppose 4 of you went for ice cream cones. How many different ways could the 4 of you line up? Can you work that out so you get 24? It's true that 4! equals 24.

Whew!

I could sure use some ice cream!

Figuring out how many ways there are to line up if there are five of you is an even bigger task. It can be done, and you might like to try it. But mathematicians are the kind of people who would rather look for the easy way to do something, even if it takes twice as long.

It's no use working out all the ways for five people to line up,

a mathematician might say,

because then I'll be stuck working out how many ways six can line up, and then seven, and so on. If I figure out a way to work the five-in-a-line problem, I'll have a method to use for any number.

Time to back up and think like a mathematician. With one person, there is only one way to line up, so 1! equals 1. With two people, there are two ways to line up, so 2! equals 2. Here's all the information so far.

1! = 1
2! = 2
3! = 6
4! = 24

And it turns out that, as in all of mathematics, there's a pattern for getting each of these with some simple arithmetic.

$$1! = 1 = 1$$
$$2! = 2 = 1 \times 2$$
$$3! = 6 = 1 \times 2 \times 3$$
$$4! = 24 = 1 \times 2 \times 3 \times 4$$

According to this pattern, to figure 5!, multiply 1 x 2 x 3 x 4 x 5, which is 120. Try 6! this way to see if you get 720.

Back to the ice cream line. It's not that ice cream has anything to do with factorial numbers. It was just an example to help you figure out how many ways there are to line up something. It's just the kind of problem that some mathematicians love. The exclamation idea is just an abbreviation. It's quicker to write 10!, for example, than to write 1 x 2 x 3 x 4 x 5 x 6 x 7 x 8 x 9 x 10; it also takes up less room than the value of 10!, which is 3,628,800. Factorial numbers get very big very fast, so the shorthand symbol comes in handy.

Here are factorials up to 15.

0!	1
1!	1
2!	2
3!	6
4!	24
5!	120
6!	720
7!	5,040
8!	40,320
9!	362,880
10!	3,628,800
11!	39,916,800
12!	479,001,600
13!	6,227,020,800
14!	87,178,291,200
15!	1,307,674,368,000

If everyone in your class at school lined up every day before going home, and there were 30 students, and you came to school every single day of the year, not even skipping weekends or holidays, it would take you almost 7 nonillion years before you had lined up every possible way. (Check page 121 for what nonillion means.) For sure, 30! is an enormous number!

One last note, for only the mathematically brave at heart. How come, on the chart above, 0! is equal to 1? Having zero people line up for ice cream cones is a ridiculous idea, and doesn't help much mathematically. But mathematicians hate to leave any idea unexplored. They do rely on patterns to help them explore ideas, and here's the pattern that has convinced mathematicians that 0! is definitely equal to 1. See if you are convinced by it. Get out your calculator.

$$6! \div 5! = 6$$
$$5! \div 4! = 5$$
$$4! \div 3! = 4$$
$$3! \div 2! = 3$$
$$2! \div 1! = 2$$

To continue this pattern, $1! \div 0! = 1$. If not, the pattern breaks down, which makes mathematicians very sad. Even nervous. That's just how mathematics works: patterns are not supposed to break down.

So 0! has to be equal to 1, because 1 divided by 1 is the only way to get 1. Can you follow this? If not, don't worry.

It may make sense to you some day. But even if it doesn't, you can still get in line for ice cream cones, whether or not you understand any factorials.

One *more* last note. If you have 15 books on a shelf and are thinking about rearranging them into all the possible lineups, you had better think twice. Even if you could rearrange them once every minute, it would take you over 2 million years to try all the possible lineups.

Lining Up

If everyone living in the 48 continental United States lined up around the border of the country, holding hands with arms outstretched, would we have enough people to go around? Would there be extras?

Some facts might help here. The border is about 12,400 miles. The average height of a person in our country is about 64 inches. And since people usually can stretch their arms to about the same distance as their height, each person would use up 64 inches of the border. And one more fact. There are about 220 million people living in the 48 states.

Heart Beating

The average person's heart beats 103,680 times a day. How many heartbeats is this in 1 minute? To find your own heartbeat rate, take your pulse for 15 seconds; multiply that by 4 to find the number of heartbeats per minute. If you don't know how to take your pulse, ask an adult to help you.

Answer to *A Mathematical Tug-of-War:*

Grandmothers will win the next and the three

Probability

Write the numbers from 1 to 4 on a piece of paper, like this:

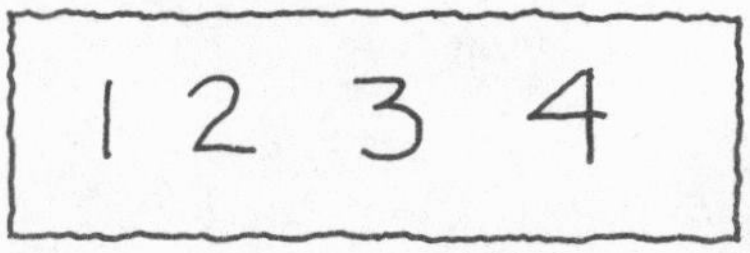
1 2 3 4

Then ask someone to circle one of the numbers. From a statistical study where this experiment was done many, many times, a mathematical theory of probability resulted: four out of five people will circle the number 3. Do you think this would be true if *you* carried out the experiment? Try it and find out.

In case your experimental subjects want to know what you're doing, tell them this:

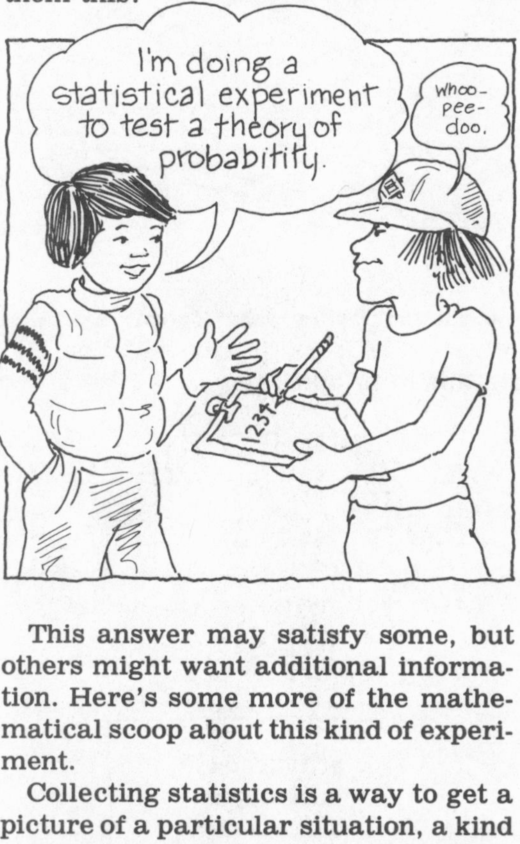
I'm doing a statistical experiment to test a theory of probabitity.
Whoo-pee-doo.
1234

This answer may satisfy some, but others might want additional information. Here's some more of the mathematical scoop about this kind of experiment.

Collecting statistics is a way to get a picture of a particular situation, a kind of numerical picture. It can be useful for predicting what is likely to happen in a situation where you don't have all the statistics. If you ask people to circle one of the numbers in the 1—2—3—4 experiment, chances are pretty good that most of them will circle the number 3; the probability is four out of five, or 4/5 as mathematicians would write it.

The "four-out-of-five" information doesn't promise that if you try the experiment on five people, four of them will circle the 3 and the other will circle one of the other numbers. Probability doesn't work like that. Probability theory *does* promise that if you do this experiment many times, the more times you try the experiment, the closer the results will come to the 4/5 probability. That's what the odds favor.

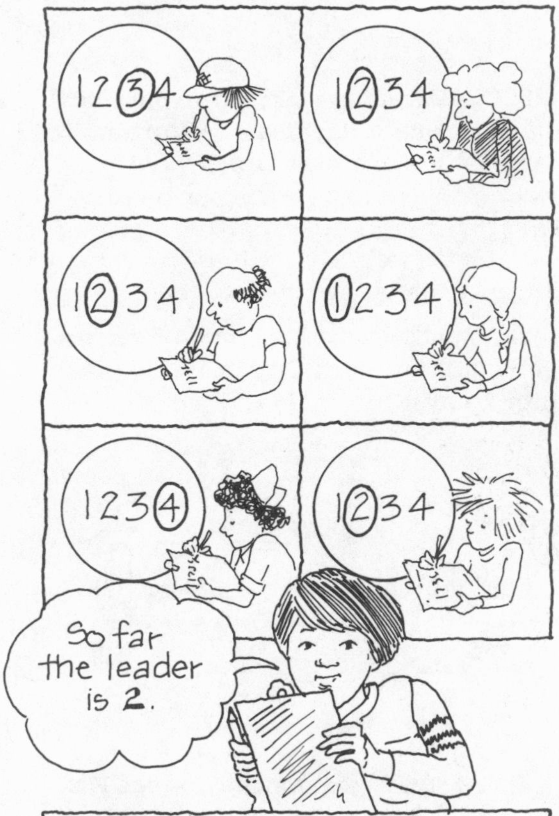
1234
1234
1234
1234
1234
1234
So far the leader is 2.

Answer to *Logical Breakfast*:
Big Eyes #5 eats banana splits for breakfast.

Cross-Country Traveling

All the following people have crossed the United States and have been written about in the *Guinness Book of World Records*. Can you match the person to the number of days?

1. In 1973 Paul Cornish peddled from San Francisco to New York City in ? days.

2. Clinton Shaw skated from New York to Santa Monica, California, in 1974. This skate took him ? days.

3. John Lees walked from Los Angeles to New York City in 1972. It took him ? days.

4. Charles Creighton and James Hargis drove their car in reverse from New York City to Los Angeles. The car they drove was a Ford Model A 1929 roadster, and they made the trip in 1930. It took them ? days.

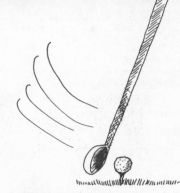

5. Floyd Satterlee Rood took 114,737 strokes to hit golf balls across the United States from the Pacific to the Atlantic. It took him ? days, and he lost 3,511 balls on the trip.

6. David Ryder went from Los Angeles to New York City on crutches. He did this in 1970 in ? days.

a. 13.22 days
b. 18 days
c. 53.51 days
d. 77 days
e. 137 days
f. 384 days

PART 6

Math Trickery

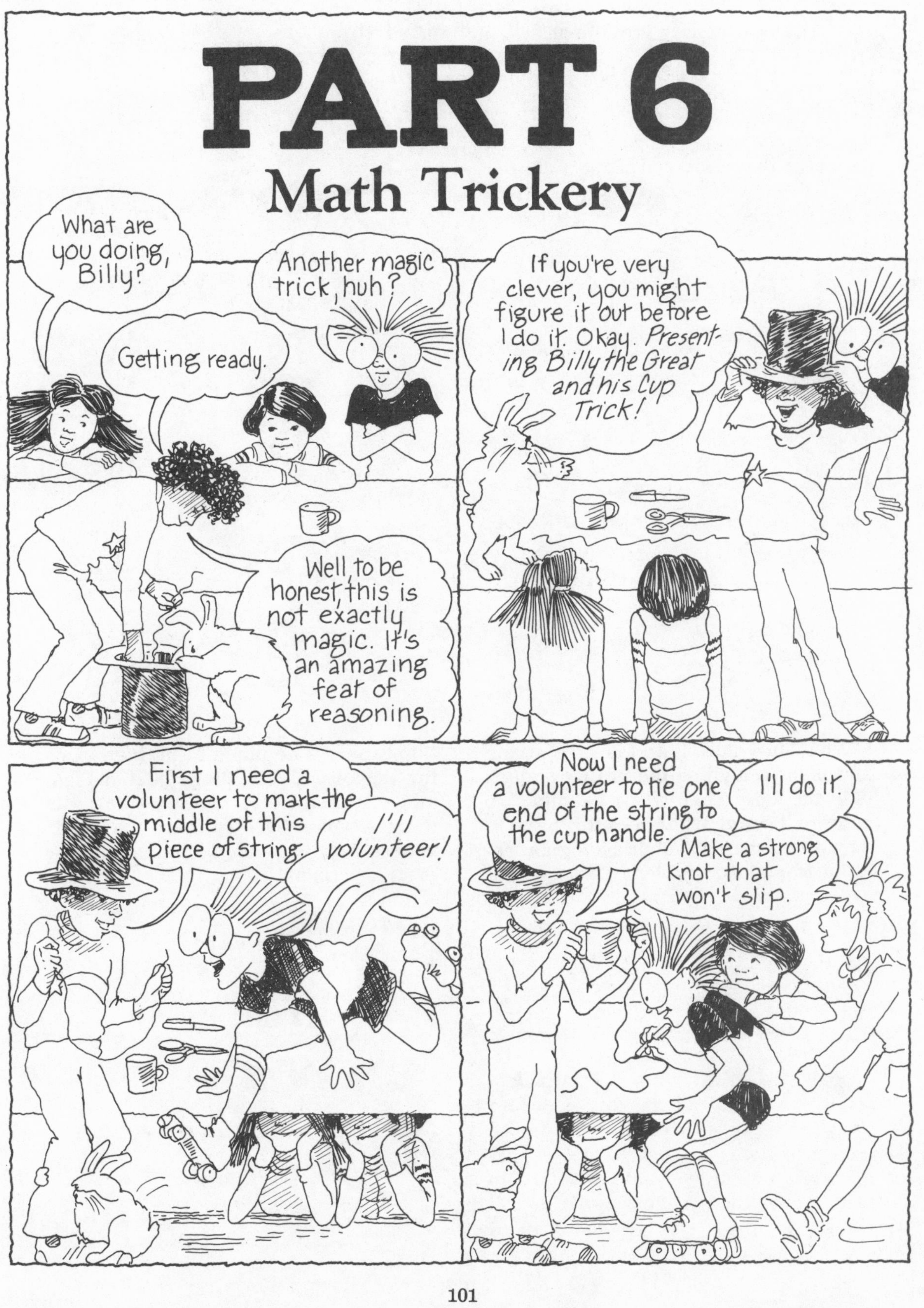

What are you doing, Billy?
Getting ready.
Another magic trick, huh?
Well, to be honest, this is not exactly magic. It's an amazing feat of reasoning.
If you're very clever, you might figure it out before I do it. Okay. *Presenting Billy the Great and his Cup Trick!*
First I need a volunteer to mark the middle of this piece of string.
I'll volunteer!
Now I need a volunteer to tie one end of the string to the cup handle.
I'll do it.
Make a strong knot that won't slip.

What Billy does is to take the string and make a knot so the halfway mark is in the loop. Then when he cuts, the cup won't drop! What does this have to do with mathematics? It's a logical solution to a tricky problem. Some people think there's no place in mathematics for trickery. Well, that's just not so, and this chapter of mathemagic aims to show you why. Try these tricks for yourself if you need convincing, or even if you don't.

The Incredible Memory Whiz

Here's a chance for a spectacular magic trick to be performed by an incredible memory whiz: you. Copy this chart on a piece of paper.

There's Billy's phone number!

(31) 2460662	(27) 8314594	(35) 6404482	(48) 9549325	(20) 1347189	(42) 3583145	(36) 7415617
(2) 3145943	(45) 6516730	(30) 1459437	(34) 5493257	(25) 6392134	(6) 7189763	(15) 6280886
(23) 4370774	(39) 0550550	(18) 9213471	(22) 3369549	(4) 5167303	(38) 9437077	(16) 7291001
(21) 2358314	(5) 6178538	(44) 5505505	(11) 2246066	(41) 2572910	(19) 0336954	(8) 9101123
(49) 0662808	(14) 5279651	(24) 5381909	(47) 8538190	(26) 7303369	(40) 1561785	(28) 9325729
(9) 0224606	(37) 8426842	(46) 7527965	(3) 4156178	(1) 2134718	(17) 8202246	(32) 3471897
(29) 0448202	(12) 3257291	(33) 4482022	(13) 4268426	(43) 4594370	(7) 8190998	(10) 1235831

Give the chart to someone. Ask that person to tell you a number in any circle, and say that you'll write the seven digits that are written below that number. That person will think you've got a pretty astounding memory—wrong. All you have to do is to use a bit of mathemagics and follow this pattern. Whatever number you're given, do this:

1. Add 11 to the number.

2. Reverse the answer you get, and write down those two numbers.

3. Add them. If the sum is less than 10, write it down. If it's greater than 10, just write down what's in the ones place.

4. Keep doing this, adding the last two numbers you get, writing down just what is in the ones place of that sum, until you get all seven digits.

Here's a sample: Suppose someone picks 49.

1. Add 11. That gives you 60.

2. Reverse the digits and write down 06, the first two of the seven digits.

3. Add 0 and 6. This gives 6. Write it down.

4. Add the 6 and 6. This gives 12. Keep only the number in the ones place, the 2. Now you have four of the digits: 0662.

5. Add 6 and 2, and write down the 8: 06628.

6. Add 2 and 8, and write just the 0. You have six of them now: 066280.

7. The last one is 8 plus 0, another 8: 0662808.

To really dazzle someone with your powers of memory, make up your own chart following this procedure, putting 12 or more digits under each circle.

Isn't That Sum-thing?

Here's one of the most dazzling answer-before-the-problem tricks. It's a truly wondrous act of addition. Ask someone in the audience for a three-digit number. Write it for all to see. Leave spaces for four more numbers and draw a line. Suppose the number you were given is 645; here's what you write.

645

On a slip of paper, after a moment of mathematical concentration, write a number and give it to someone to hold until the end of the trick. You get the number you write down by putting a 2 in front of the number you were given (2,645) and then subtracting 2 from it (2,645 - 2 = 2,643). So it's 2,643 that the person gets to hold.

You then ask for a second three-digit number; write it under the first one. Suppose you're given 473.

You write down a third number: 526.

Ask for a fourth number from the audience. Suppose it's 128.

Then you write the fifth: 871.

Now, with a little help from the audience, add up the five numbers. The answer will match the number you wrote on that slip of paper. Isn't that sum-thing?

The trick is in the two numbers you write. When you're given the second number, subtract each digit from 9 to write the third. Do the same with the fourth to get the fifth. This way the sum of each of the last two pairs of numbers adds up to 999. So you're really adding 999 twice, for a total of 1,998, to whatever number you were given to start with. That you know ahead of time. Well, 1,998 is 2,000 minus 2. That's why you have to add the 2 in front (in the thousands place) and subtract 2 from the original number. (What would the answer be if you have the audience pick a sixth number, and you pick a seventh before the final addition?)

The Calendar Caper

You'll need a month from an old calendar for this trick. Have someone draw around a square block of numbers, four by four.

When that has been done, you write a number on a slip of paper and hand it to someone to hold. Then you turn your back and give these instructions:

1. Circle any one date in the blocked-off square.
2. Cross out all the other numbers in the row and column that the circled number is in.
3. Now circle another number.
4. Again cross out the other numbers in the row and column the second number is in.
5. Do this again for a third number.
6. There should be only one date left that isn't circled or crossed out. Circle it.
7. Add up the circled dates.

Then you ask the person holding the slip of paper to read the number on it. It's the same as the total of the circled numbers!

To get the correct number to write on the slip of paper, you add the dates of two opposite corners and double the sum. This magic will work for any square block this size on any month.

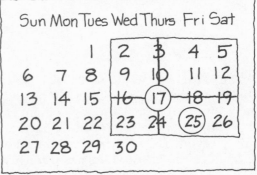

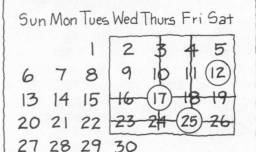

Calculator Tricks

Announce that you are very fortunate because the calculator you have not only adds, subtracts, multiplies, and divides, but it helps you do magic as well. Then proceed to use it to help you do these tricks.

The Favorite-Number Trick. Give someone the magic calculator and have him (suppose it's a boy) punch in this number: thirty-seven thousand thirty-seven. Then check to see that the calculator reads 37,037. Ask him for his favorite number between 1 and 9. Whatever number he gives you, multiply it by 3 in your head, and tell him to multiply what he has already put into the calculator by that number. If he says 4 is his favorite number, for example, tell him to multiply by 12. If he says 7, he needs to multiply by 21. What he'll get is an answer that's a row of his favorite number.

The Three-Dice Trick. You need three dice as well as your magic calculator. Get someone in the audience to roll the dice. You, with the help of your calculator, will guess the three numbers that came up. After the dice are rolled, give someone the calculator and give these instructions:

1. Multiply the number on one of the dice by 2.
2. Add 5.
3. Multiply this result by 5.
4. Add a number from one of the other two dice.
5. Now multiply by 10.
6. Add the third number.
7. Give back the calculator.

You subtract 250. There will be a three-digit number. The three digits will be the numbers that came up on the dice.

The Guess-the-Card Trick. Ask someone to pick any card from the deck. Everyone should see it except for you. Your job is to guess that card, with the help of your magic calculator. Give the person who picked the card the calculator and give these directions:

1. Punch in the card number (ace = 1, jack = 11, queen = 12, king = 13).
2. Multiply that number by 2.
3. Add 1.
4. Multiply by 5.
5. Add another number depending on which suit the card is: clubs = 6, diamonds = 7, hearts = 8, spades = 9.
6. Ask to see the calculator with the answer showing.

Whatever number is now on the calculator, subtract 5 from it. The tens place of your final answer tells the number of the card. The ones place tells the suit according to the numbers above.

Here's an example: Let's suppose someone picks the 8 of clubs. Eight is punched in. Multiply it by 2 for 16. Adding 1 gives 17. Multiply by 5 for 85. Add six since it's a club, and that brings the number to 91. The calculator shows 91. You subtract 5 and get 86. The 8 is the number of the card; the 6 tells you that it's a club. Presto!

Getting Your Money's Worth

Which would you rather have: your weight in dimes or your weight in half dollars? Would you make the same choice if you were offered a barrel of dimes or a barrel of half dollars if both barrels were the same size?

Answers to *Cross-Country Traveling:*
1-g, 5-g, 3-c, 4-p, 2-t, e-6

The Magic Touch

This card trick requires that you wear something with a pocket large enough to hold a deck of cards. Here's how the trick looks to the audience. Someone shuffles the cards, which you put into your pocket. Then you ask someone to name any one card from the deck. Suppose the 6 of diamonds is named. You reach into your pocket and take out a card that is a diamond, checking with the audience to see that you have the right suit. Then you reach in again and pull out a 4 and a 2 and ask if the sum of these two is the same as the chosen card. What a touch!

one with the correct suit. Suppose this time the card named was the jack of spades. You've already drawn out the 8 of spades to show the suit. Now you need to pull out the cards that add up to 11: ace, 2, and 8 do it. You already have the 8, so pull out the ace and 2 and you tell the audience to total all three cards to get the correct number. If it had been the jack of hearts that had been named, you wouldn't need the 4 of hearts after you used it to show the suit. In that case you just discard it and pull out the other three. Once in a while, someone will name one of the four magic cards, then you really show some magic.

Do 4 and 2 add up to the chosen card?

Neat.

Where does he get these tricks?

These cards go in your pocket beforehand.

To get ready for this trick remove four cards from the deck before you give it to the audience and put these four in your pocket in an order that you have memorized. The four cards are the ace of clubs, the 2 of diamonds, the 4 of hearts, and the 8 of spades. In this order the numbers go from smallest to largest and the suits are in alphabetical order. The order isn't important, as long as you can reach in and pull out any one you want at any time. Practice this ahead of time.

Now, when the deck is shuffled, put it in your pocket without disturbing the four cards already there. When you're told the card, reach in and pick out the

What about the four secret cards? Having one of each suit is essential for being able to pull out the correct suit. But why the ace, 2, 4, and 8? That's because you can make any number up to 15 by adding different combinations of those four numbers. Here's a chart that shows how. A checkmark indicates that a number is being used.

8	4	2	1	
			✓	1
		✓		2
		✓	✓	3
	✓			4
	✓		✓	5
	✓	✓		6
	✓	✓	✓	7
✓				8
✓			✓	9
✓		✓		10
✓		✓	✓	11
✓	✓			12
✓	✓		✓	13

These are the only four numbers that will work. Notice that each one is a double of the one smaller than it is, two times as large. Mathematicians call these numbers the "powers of two."

★ $1 SENTENCE ★

Kristen imported raincoats wholesale.

Answer to King Arthur's Problem: There's only one number that is the same — 45 976.

Answer to Who's Who?: Joshua is 11, and Rachel is 13. Maria is 9, Great Old Mark is 10.

Here's the answer to **Quick Change**.

The Force Is with You

Here's another mathemagic trick you can perform for several friends. Give them each a slip of paper and ask them to write their names on one side. Collect the papers.

Then ask each of them to think of a number from 51 to 100. Tell them to concentrate on the numbers they've chosen so you can get their thoughts.

Ask them to concentrate quietly so "the force" can be with you. While they're doing this, you write a number on each of their slips of paper, on the blank side, and then fold them so only their names are showing.

When you have done this, tell them to each add a certain number you give them to their own. You give the same number to all of them. Then they each cross out the left-hand digit in their answer and add that digit to what's left of the number. When you hand each of them the folded paper with their name on it, the number they now have is written inside.

How can you be so clever? Well, first of all, they'll all wind up with the same answer. The mathemagic takes care of that. Writing the numbers on different slips of paper just adds to their amazement.

Here's what you do. Pick a number from 1 to 50 that you'd like them all to finally get and write that on each slip. In your head subtract your number from 99. Say the result out loud. That's the number they add to their thought number. Suppose you picked 26 and wrote that on their slips of paper. Subtract 26 from 99 and you get 73. They each add 73 to their number.

Suppose someone picked the number 65. Adding 73 gives 138. Cross out the left-hand digit, the 1, and add that to what's left, the 38. That gives 39. Subtract 39 from the original 65, and that leaves 26, the number you've already written. If you suspect that some in your audience might not be too terrific in arithmetic, have them work in pairs, each pair giving you one slip. (Or let them borrow your magic calculator.) The real force, of course, is mathematics!

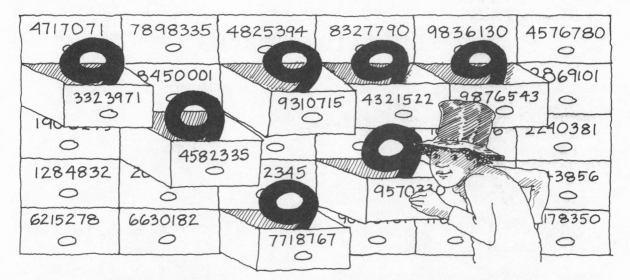

You Always Get Nine

Take any number at all, with as many digits as you like. (Your telephone number is as good as any to start with.) Write down your number. Then scramble those digits any way you'd like.

Subtract the smaller from the larger of these two numbers. Whatever answer you get, add up the digits in it. And whatever sum you get from this, add those digits again. And keep adding them until you wind up with just one number. It will be a 9.

Here's an example. Suppose you start with 4572738. Rearrange them to this: 8747523. Subtract: 8747523 - 4574738 = 4174785. Add up those digits: 4 + 1 + 7 + 4 + 7 + 8 + 5. That sum is 36. And add the 3 and the 6; you get 9.

This will work every time. It doesn't matter what number you start with. It doesn't matter how you rearrange them. Add this to your collection of mathemagic.

★ $1 SENTENCE ★

Thirty costumed starfish merrily performed.

Metric Eyesight

Having 20-20 vision means that your eyes are in great shape. A person with 20-20 vision can read a certain line on an eye chart that is placed 20 feet away. What's going to happen in the eye doctor's office when the metric system takes over?

I'll see farther?

Guess again.

The Three Sacks

The three little pig eyes have a few standard tricks to fall back on when things get a bit slow. This does happen to them from time to time. It's one of the regular patterns of life as a trickster. (If you have never heard of the three little pig eyes and are wondering what this is all about, you may want to check the tale on page 22 for a proper introduction to this strange trio.)

The three little pig eyes always keep their eyes open (as wide as they can, that is) for fairs and carnivals. Being magical creatures, it's easy for them to sneak in, open a booth, and not be noticed as being strange. Well, at least not *too* strange.

One of their favorite booths to set up at fairs and carnivals is the three sacks booth. It's quick and simple. They have three sacks of things and charge people to guess what's in each. The people who guess right get a prize.

Here's one they set up last summer at a carnival. Their sign was a real grabber: Pay a nickel to win a quarter! Increase your 5 cents by 500 percent.

T.J. was one of the customers who got interested. One trickster explained to him what was in the three sacks: "Money, money, they're full of money. There are nickels and quarters, and I'm not being funny." Then it pointed to the sacks and continued the rhyme, "One sack has quarters; another has nickels; the third sack, however, is really a tickle. It's a mixture of both, a fair share of each; finding which sack is which is within your reach." (The pig eyes never claimed to be great poets.)

This got T.J. interested, but he was also pretty confused. You see, each of the sacks was clearly labeled. One was labeled "Nickels"; one was labeled "Quarters"; and the third was labeled "Nickels and Quarters." So it seemed like no problem at all to find out which sack was which. But you must remember that the three little pig eyes are tricky creatures, and things are rarely as they seem when you are around them.

At this point, with T.J. even more interested, another of the pig eyes explained further. "The labels aren't right," this trickster said. "It wouldn't be much of a trick if you just paid your nickel and told us which sack had which coins in it and then got a quarter. We'd be out of quarters in no time."

T.J. was willing. "I'll take a chance," he said. The three little pig eyes snapped into action.

"That will be one nickel, please," one pig eyes said.

Then another explained, "One clue is that each of the sacks is labeled incorrectly; you can be sure about that."

That's when the third pig eyes chimed in. "But we don't expect you merely to guess. We give you clues. Two clues. And with the two clues, you can definitely figure out which sack is which—with some clever thinking, that is."

Then the third trickster finished. "You get your second clue this way: Pick any one sack, and we'll reach in and pick out one coin and show you what it is."

Which sack would you reach into?

With this explanation, T.J. decided to go for it. Then he got the details of the problem. "I've got two and a half dozen coins," one of the pig eyes said slyly. "All totaled, I've got 32 cents. What are the coins?"

T.J. won. (Actually, people won pretty often. Especially the ones who were math smarty pants.) So then the little pig eyes, tricksters that they were, came up with another offer. It went something like this.

"Say," one of them said to T.J., "would you like a chance to double your winnings?"

"How?" T.J. asked.

"It's another problem. I tell you how many coins I have in my pocket and how much they're worth all together. If you can figure out what the coins are, I'll give you another quarter. If not, you give me back the quarter you won."

115

Then to cheer up T.J., the little pig eyes gave him a riddle, for free, that he could try on someone else. They might be tricksters, but they are basically good-natured creatures. The riddle was written on a card:

Why are 1966 pennies worth almost $20?

Because 1966 pennies are worth $19.66, only 34¢ less than $20.

What am I doing here??

T.J. started to think. And think. He took out a pencil. (The pig eyes cheerfully supplied paper.) He could not figure it out, however. And he didn't feel very well when he found out what the answer was! You see, this was one of the trick questions the three little pig eyes love. It wasn't a fair-and-square problem like the three-sacks problem. This one had a trick to it. But then again, what can you expect from tricksters? Can you figure out the answer?

PART 7
Thinking Big

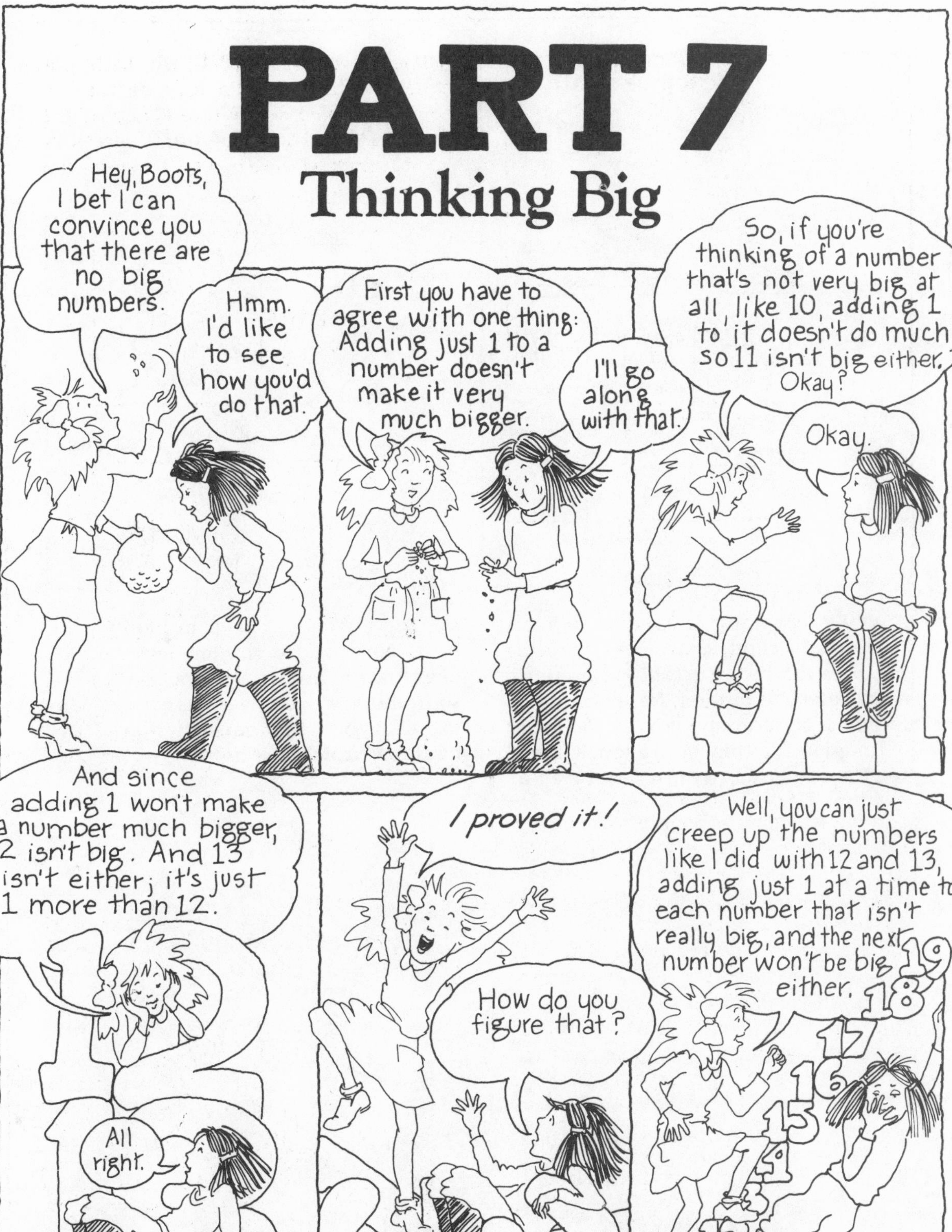

Hey, Boots, I bet I can convince you that there are no big numbers.
Hmm. I'd like to see how you'd do that.
First you have to agree with one thing: Adding just 1 to a number doesn't make it very much bigger.
I'll go along with that.
So, if you're thinking of a number that's not very big at all, like 10, adding 1 to it doesn't do much, so 11 isn't big either. Okay?
Okay.
And since adding 1 won't make a number much bigger, 12 isn't big. And 13 isn't either; it's just 1 more than 12.
All right.
I proved it!
How do you figure that?
Well, you can just creep up the numbers like I did with 12 and 13, adding just 1 at a time to each number that isn't really big, and the next number won't be big either.

You see, according to this, no number will ever be considered a big number. It will just be 1 more than the one before it. That proves it.

There's something wrong here. It's logical, but it's not right. I know it's just not right.

968,321,055   968,321,056

968,321,0_5_56

Sally's reasoning may seem logical, but Boots is right. Sally isn't correct. Numbers can be big, too big to imagine even. Take one million, for example. A million of something is really too large to imagine. If this entire book were filled with words, with no pictures at all, there wouldn't be a million words in it. Not even a million letters. Not even half a million letters. So there's something wrong with Sally's reasoning. Can you figure out what it is? Maybe this chapter will help.

I say Sally's been hanging around those pig eyes too much.

How Big Is Big?

Suppose you tried to count to 1,000,000 and counted just one number each second, without taking out any time for eating or sleeping or even practicing the piano. How long would it take? A calculator helps to figure out this one. Start like this: There are 60 seconds in a minute, and 60 minutes in an hour, so that makes 3,600 seconds in an hour. There are 24 hours in a day, which means there are 86,400 seconds in a day. You take it from there.

Students in Sherwood Bates Elementary School in Raleigh, North Carolina, were learning what 1,000,000 looked like firsthand, at least in bottle caps. They started collecting bottle caps in September. By March they had 787,000, which meant almost a quarter of a million still to go. That's when a snag developed. What were they going to do with all those bottle caps? Already what they had collected would fill about 150 *large* boxes!

The Sherwood Bates students finally made it, with a grand total of more than 1,170,000 bottle caps. And North Carolina solved their problem of what to do with the caps—they bought them for recycling. The Mayor of Raleigh declared June 13, 1980, as Bank-a-Million Day.

What about 1,000,000 days? How many years would that be? Will you be alive a million days from now?

Would 1,000,000 pennies fit in your bedroom? One million pennies weigh over 3 tons. Could your bedroom hold that weight? (How much are 1,000,000 pennies worth anyway?)

If you had a cylindrical tank big enough to hold 1,000,000 glasses of milk, it would need to be 75 feet high and 10 feet in diameter.

Can you imagine how big 1,000,000 really is?

Mathematical Abbreviations

To write one million as a numeral takes a 1 and six 0's: 1,000,000. To write one billion, you use a 1 and nine 0's: 1,000,000,000. One trillion uses three more 0's: 1,000,000,000,000.

Large numbers have always been interesting to mathematicians. Writing lots of zeros isn't so interesting. There's a way to write abbreviations for large numbers, without all those zeros. One million (1,000,000) can be written 10^6. One billion (1,000,000,000) is 10^9. One trillion (1,000,000,000,000) is 10^{12}. The little number is the same as the number of zeros, and is called an "exponent." An exponent tells how many times to multiply the other number, called the "base," by itself. So 10^6 equals 10 x 10 x 10 x 10 x 10 x 10, and that equals 1,000,000. (You can check that on your calculator.)

$$100 = 10^2 (10 \times 10)$$
$$1{,}000 = 10^3 (10 \times 10 \times 10)$$
$$10{,}000 = 10^4 (10 \times 10 \times 10 \times 10)$$
$$100{,}000 = 10^5 (10 \times 10 \times 10 \times 10 \times 10)$$

All of these numbers are called "powers of ten." To read any one of them, such as 1,000, you can say "one thousand," or "ten to the third power." One million is "ten to the sixth power."

With numbers that aren't exactly a power of ten, 13 million (13,000,000), for example, mathematicians use a shorthand that still uses exponents with ten as the base. Since 13 million is 13 times 1 million, you can write it as 13 x 10^6. That's a standard abbreviation called "scientific notation." You'll probably run across this in school sometime, if you haven't already. Remember, an abbreviation is useful to you only if you understand where it came from and what it means!

More Mathematical Abbreviations

Exponents are especially useful when the powers of ten get even bigger. Here's a chart that shows how handy mathematical shorthand can be.

Power of Ten	Number name
10^3	Thousand
10^6	Million
10^9	Billion
10^{12}	Trillion
10^{15}	Quadrillion
10^{18}	Quintillion
10^{21}	Sextillion
10^{24}	Septillion
10^{27}	Octillion
10^{30}	Nonillion
10^{33}	Decillion
10^{36}	Undecillion
10^{39}	Duodecillion
10^{42}	Tredecillion
10^{45}	Quattuordecillion
10^{48}	Quindecillion
10^{51}	Sexdecillion
10^{54}	Septendecillion
10^{57}	Octodecillion
10^{60}	Novemdecillion
10^{63}	Vigintillion
10^{100}	Googol

Can you figure out what number name fits 10^8? Or 10^{10}?

Which Is Bigger? One million billion or one billion million? Can you write each of these as a power of ten?

Answers to the *Pizza Problems*:

#1: The time would be a quarter to two. #5: The other half. #3: He was not hungry enough for two. #4: Cut it in half! Stack the two halves on top of each other. Cut this pile in half again. Now you have four pieces. Stack them on top of each other and cut in half again to get eight pieces. #2: Alicia's favorite pizza is mushroom, Mike's is sausage, Patrick's is anchovy, and Sara's is pepperoni! #6: There are 105 different pizzas with two ingredients each. #7: Ten minutes.

Powers Other Than Ten

You don't have to use exponents just for powers of ten. You can have powers of two, three, or of any number. The rule is still the same: The exponent tells how many times to multiply the base by itself. So 2^6 means $2 \times 2 \times 2 \times 2 \times 2 \times 2$, which is 64. And 6^2 means 6×6, or 36.

Which of these pairs is more?

$$2^3 \text{ or } 3^2$$
$$2^4 \text{ or } 4^2$$
$$2^5 \text{ or } 5^2$$

Do you notice a pattern about these? Is that pattern true for other bases and exponents?

The Fifth Powers. It has been said that the fifth power of a number always ends in the last digit of the base number. For example, $2^5 = 32$ and $13^5 = 371{,}293$. Test this for others.

121

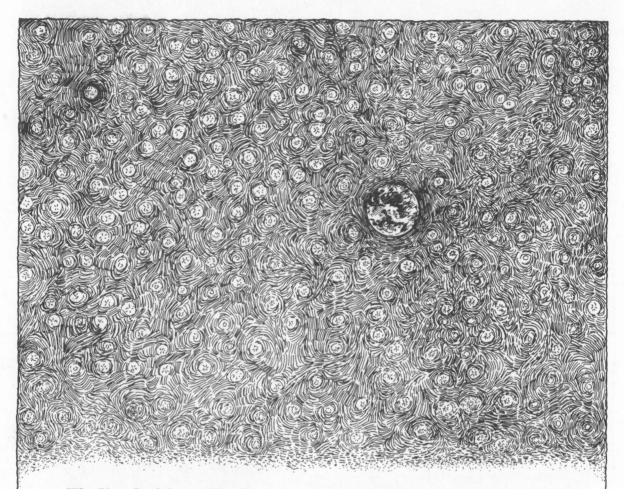

Who Uses Such Large Numbers Anyway?

If such large numbers are so hard to imagine, why bother with them? For some people they're very important. Astronomers, for example. You may have learned about the speed of light in school; light travels at 186,000 miles per second. The sun is 93,000,000 miles away from Earth (more or less—at that distance a few miles doesn't make much difference). So it takes the light from the sun about 8 minutes to reach the Earth.

How far does light travel in 1 year? There are 86,400 seconds in 1 day, and just about 365¼ days in a year. So in 1 year, light travels 186,000 x 86,400 x 365¼ miles. This is about 6,000,000,000,-000 (6×10^{12}) miles (more or less). You can read that as "six trillion miles" or "six times ten to the twelfth power miles." But instead of either of those, that distance is called "one light year." Can you explain why?

A light year is an incredibly long distance, much too long to visualize. But scientists know that many stars are much farther away from Earth than that, and that a light year really isn't so terribly far when you're thinking about the universe. Polaris is the North Star, the one at the end of the handle of the Little Dipper. It is 300 light years away from Earth. That means that on any night you're looking at that star, the light you see is the way Polaris looked 300 years ago! Some of the stars you see at night don't even exist anymore; they've already died, but their light is just now getting to Earth.

A Speedy Problem

For this problem you need to know two speeds. Light travels fast: 186,000 miles per second. Sound travels fast, but not as fast: 1,100 feet per second.

Suppose you're at a rock concert, sitting 100 feet from the band. The concert is being broadcast on the radio, and someone is listening to it 1,000 miles away. Radio waves travel at the speed of light. Who will hear the music first—you or the radio listener?

Worldwide News

Suppose a baby was born at midnight, and you told one person about this new baby. Then that person told two others within 10 minutes. And then those two each told two others in 10 minutes. And this continued all night long, with every person telling two others every 10 minutes who hadn't yet been told. How many people would know by 8 o'clock in the morning?

Answers to The Three Sacks: the correct sack to reach into is the one labeled "Nickels and Quarters." I knew that. But with the second problem, I did not figure out that there were two pennies and six nickels in the big ones, pocket dozen nickels were the half dozen coins in the problem, and the two pennies were the other two. See why it was a trick question!

The Million-Dollar Giveaway

If you had $1,000,000 (don't you wish?), and you decided to give away $50 every hour, how long would it take you to give away the total amount? How old would you be then?

Math on the Beach. If you look at a 1-mile stretch of beach that is 100 feet wide and 1 foot deep, you're looking at 10^{14} grains of sand. That's one hundred trillion, and nothing to sneeze at.

Some Numbers Are
More Perfect Than Others

I'm sure *they* realized the error of their ways. Euclid, that dear boy, one of the most spectacular of the Greeks, wrote about me and some of my perfect friends in the first century B.C. He appreciated us, not only because we are so perfect, but because he knew how rare we are.

It was no easy task to find us. After me comes 28. And the third comes a long way after; it's 496. The fourth is 8,128. It took mathematicians over 1,500 years to find the fifth perfect number. It was a toughie, a real hideout: 33,550,336. And it has only been since the invention of the electronic computing machines that they have found the next one: 8,589,869,056. Oh, we're a rare collection. (But I'm first and always will be.)

Being perfect isn't easy, I'll have you know. It's hard to find friends of my quality. After all, there just aren't too many perfect numbers around. I'm the smallest of all of us; and I was the first one discovered. The Greeks found me, for which I'm grateful. Deeply grateful.

Those Greeks were extraordinary fellows. They felt that we perfect numbers are rather mystical. Some felt we were slightly nonsensical as well, but

I'm sure you're wondering what makes us so very perfect. It has to do with our proper divisors, you see, the numbers which are smaller than we are and divide into us evenly. For each of us absolutely perfect numerical wonders, our proper divisors add up to us, exactly. Take me for instance. My proper divisors are 1, 2, and 3. (Not 4, or 5, since they don't divide into me evenly. I've always detested leftovers.) And if you add 1, 2, and 3, you get me, 6. It's just perfect.

That simply marvelous property doesn't occur again until 28. The divisors of 28 are 1, 2, (not 3), 4, (not 5 or 6), 7, and 14. Just those five. You can check for yourself that they add up to 28.

If you're one of those doubting types (and I certainly hope you are—doubters are so much more exciting as thinkers), check out 496.

I was at a party recently. I can't remember where the party was—I'm invited to *so* many. Well, there was a 10 just preening for a group of admirers.

"What's going on here?" I whispered to a friend.

"Well," she said, "they all think that 10 is absolutely perfect. After all, it has done so much for place value and is a perfect match for people's fingers and toes."

"What?" I said, a bit louder than I had meant to, I'm afraid. Well, I just couldn't contain myself. This was an impostor of the worst sort. Now 10 may have some interesting characteristics (though I've never really noticed them myself), but being perfect is definitely not one of them. Even the mathematicians agree. Check its perfect divisors for yourself. The only numbers smaller than 10 that divide into it evenly are 1, 2, and 5. Add those and all you get is 8.

Hardly 10. And when a number's proper divisors add up to less than itself, it's given a most appropriate label. The mathematicians call those numbers "deficient," and I agree with them wholeheartedly.

Now there are some numbers that aren't perfect, but they aren't deficient either. Take 12, for example. Its proper divisors are 1, 2, 3, 4, and 6. Add those up, and you get a hefty sum: 16. (Some numbers have just let themselves go.) "Abundant" is what mathematicians call these numbers, a rather polite label for such chubby entities.

We perfect numbers have dazzled mathematicians for ages. For example, they've noticed that all of us are even. Well, of course! What did you expect? But those mathematicians are doubters. Darlings, but doubters. They like to prove things, and they've been trying for simply ages to prove that an odd number can't be perfect, but none of them has done it yet! They just don't come like Euclid anymore!

Before I go, dear readers, I have a question for you. How old are you? Is your age perfect or abundant or deficient?

And one more thing — *if* you can imagine this at all — the seventeenth perfect number has 1,373 digits in it! Talk about perfection!

MATH TALK

In mathematics, easy words sometimes stand for not-so-easy ideas. And that can be confusing. You know the words, but you don't necessarily know what the mathematical meanings for them are.

Take the word "perfect" for an example. Think about what the word perfect means to you. Check it in the dictionary. Now can you see any reason why the number 28 ought to be called perfect? Check page 124 to find out. It doesn't have much to do with what "perfect" means in a nonmathematical sense.

If you feel positive, or negative, about something, that's a sign of your attitude. Not so in mathematics. Positive and negative numbers aren't cheerful or grumpy. Positive numbers are larger than zero, and negative numbers are smaller than zero, and that's all there is to that.

An odd number isn't terribly unusual, it just isn't even. Hardly enough excuse to be called odd in English, but perfectly understandable in mathematics!

There are other such words: table, plot, function, product, times, power. And lots more. It's as if some words have one meaning in English and an entirely different meaning in mathematics.

Some of learning mathematics has to do with understanding ideas that have names similar to other, unrelated ideas. You need to remember that. And you need to remember that the *ideas* are the important things. The names are only as useful to you as your understanding of them.

Read the following description and see if you can figure out what is being described. It's an object that is usually found in homes where someone sews.

> A portion of a small right circular cone, made by a cut parallel to its base, convex on the crown, semiperforated with symmetrical indentations, usually congruent with a hollow interior.

It's a thimble. Aren't you glad mathematicians don't run everything in this
world?